Hiraeth

Author as Kangaroo

Helen iles navigates an outer-inner journey towards a way of being in this world that makes sense. Through her work, she aims to inspire freedom, simple living and nature awareness. Hiraeth follows on from her well-loved series of eco-documentaries:
 - Ecovillage Pioneers (50 min) 2009
 - Lammas (50 min) 2012
 - Deep Listening (60 min) 2015

Hiraeth is an invitation to live a more connected way of being. Awake and in accordance to our inner compass.

HIRAETH

Our Longing for Belonging

Helen iles

© Simply Living Project 2019

Hiraeth by Helen iles
www.hiraethbook.org

© Simply Living Project 2019
All rights reserved

Cover photography © Natasha Brooks
https://tashbrooks.com

All other images © Helen iles

This book or any portion thereof may not be reproduced or used in any manner whatsoever without the express written permission of the publisher except for the use of brief quotations in a book review.

ISBN 978-1-9162859-1-0

Printed in the UK by
Simply Living Project Ltd
27, Old Gloucester Street
LONDON
WC1N 3AX

For all my relations
in all their forms

Contents

Foreword		9
1	Leaving	15
2	The Land Owns Me	21
3	The Things we do for Love	29
4	Connecting the Dots	35
5	Not the End of Suburbia	47
6	A Home Economy	55
7	Conflict and Resolution	65
8	Always Was	71
9	Dispossessed	77
10	Neighbours	83
11	Deep Listening	93

12	At the Centre of it All	101
13	Becalmed	107
14	The Husband's Tale	113
15	Villa Mimosa	117
16	What the World Needs Now	129
17	Walking On	139
	Afterword	147
	Notes and Resources	149

Moonprint by Natasha Brooks

Foreword

"Hiraeth - this beautiful, soulful word, is much more than a longing for home. It is a longing for belonging."

It began with a feeling of being lost. A feeling, if you are Welsh, you might describe as *hiraeth*. *Hiraeth* is one of the few Welsh language words which resonates through English-speaking Wales as well. The Welsh claim that it is untranslatable, but is understood to speak of a longing for one's homeland and is often interpreted as homesickness. I want to suggest that the word has a deeper meaning than that. That Cymraeg - this ancient language of poetry and myth - lends *hiraeth* a more mystical significance than a mere longing for one's country. As well as a longing for land, I sense that it points to a disconnection of spirit. A severance from that part of the self that lives behind the eyes, beyond the seen. If we cut a human body open, we won't find spirit but still, if the spirit leaves, we somehow know it, and not only at the time of death. To be 'spirited' is to be lively - *lifely*, but to be dispirited, is to be lacking in life. *Theos*, the greek word for god, is embedded in the word enthusiasm, and it is interesting to note how enthusiasm - a kind of liveliness or vivacity - was discredited along with other aspects of religion during the age of reason, ironically known as the Age of Enlightenment. Reason-able people saw it as a kind of mania - far from the seriousness required in proper behaviour.

As focus shifted from belief and faith to that which could be proven, science became the new god and in the process, we lost taste for knowledge that came through our felt senses. Rational thought gained precedence over inner knowing. Prayer lost its power and intuition became something unreliable, not to be trusted. In this powerful over-writing can be seen the domination of masculine over feminine - a deference for objective truth over subjective feelings; for independence over the relational. Logic over feelings paved the way for the industrial revolution, where the natural world - and humans alongside it - became little more than a convenient resource. It is this materialist, elitist view which now leads us, as humans and as a living planet, through a time of mass extinction, as we destroy the natural habitats on which we depend on and imprison souls in life-denying edifices of concrete and glass. Focusing exclusively on the material, ignoring the wholeness of existence, we disconnect ourselves from the animating force - the creative spirit. Intuition and imagination lean toward madness and in some way, witless. But the origin of both wit and wise is in the Old English *witan* and German *wissen* - to know, and also in an Indo-European root giving us Latin's *videre*, meaning 'see'. Is it possible that those with experiences which society calls nonsensical, illogical, irrational or simply wrong have access to a different kind of knowing or seeing? And that when we fail to validate that experience - either unknowingly (unwittingly) or deliberately, through practices such as gaslighting, we undermine a person's experience in such a way as to make them appear (and feel) insane?

Amidst rocketing global mental ill-health, let us look again at the way we live our lives and make time and space for the knowing that comes via the felt senses. For the wisdom that goes beyond the material. The mindfulness movement has brought us tools that enable a slowing down and noticing, but it takes more than a calming of our overworked, exhausted alarm systems. It takes a deep dive into the inner world, an understanding of the ways we can address and engage with, instead of ignoring, sidestepping or escaping. We need to find a way to discover what that the buddhists might call refuge, a sense of safety found not only in land and community, though they surely support it. A refuge is a place where we can truly rest.

FOREWORD

Where we can be ourselves and feel accepted and loved.

Hiraeth has us longing for this place. A place that we could call a home for the spirit. A spiritual home. A home inside.

Born into at least three generations of Welsh and having lived all my life in that country, at the age of forty-five I left on an adventure. I was homesick, of course, but it wasn't until I had spent three years in Australia and almost one further year living in Spain, that I sniffed the scent of this deeper meaning of *hiraeth*. For the first time ever I was suffering from extreme anxiety. Wandering around Barcelona under a cloud, the bell jar that Sylvia Plath used to describe her depression suddenly made sense.[1] I felt isolated from other people and from the place I found myself living. I lacked the tools with which to navigate my new life. When I looked around for calming nature, I found only hard angles. When I craved silence, there was none to be found. It made sense that someone so used to a rural quiet would find city life difficult, but still it was hard to accept I was failing. Surely my many years as a yoga and meditation teacher should have helped me cope? Ashamed, I retreated, numbing myself against the shrieking of my senses. I was still imagining that I could hide my dislocated state when a friend told me, in a quiet voice, that she believed I had "lost my spirit."

Like a well-meaning dose of shock therapy, my friend's simple, honest statement initiated my journey back to lifely-ness, but the effect was far from immediate. Despite acknowledging that there was indeed a problem, fear had me stuck - unable to make meaningful movement in any direction and yet unable to muster the trust required for true surrender. When I finally was able to look up from my own pain, I couldn't help noticing how many people had similar symptoms. Anxiety. Restlessness. Depression. Statistics bear it out. These are the dis-eases of our modern age. [2]
It struck me then how the ancient language of Wales had put its eloquent finger right on the essence of it. *Hiraeth* - this beautiful, soulful word, is

much more than a longing for home. It is a longing for belonging, for connection and for love. It is a longing for a reunion with the very source of ourselves. With creativity and inspiration. It is a longing for life itself and for a relationship with the divine in all its forms. It is no accident that the practice of mindfulness, which is dressed up as secular but which in reality is all about the spiritual, invites us to feel. Feel the body. Feel the sensations. Feel the emotions. Reconnect with the whole of who you are. With yourself, with your environment, with other people. Let the feeling lead you to knowing, but not from a place of thinking. Not from a place of rationalising. Mindfulness invites us to simply know what we know and respond, as best we can, from there. Try as it might, with its talk of seratonin and flight-or-flight 'mechanisms', to sneak in under the rational guise of neuroscience, mindfulness speaks the language of spirit and to soul. No wonder we've all gone crazy for it.

The journey of this book, which takes us to the other side of the world (and back), draws on my personal practice of mindfulness, meditation and yoga and my contact with teachers of buddhadharma, from which the tools of mindfulness are borrowed. It is a reflection on the nature of community - *sangha* - and how our modern ways of living and being often fail to support a connection to people and place. Along the way I encounter permaculture, both as a system of design and a way of engaging with land and others. I am also strongly influenced by wisdom from perhaps the only unbroken culture on this planet - the Australian Aboriginal culture - which finds me learning how to bring about healing through the practice of deep listening. This journey, then, is a soul journey, with all the play of light and dark that this suggests. Will you join me?

Gower, Wales

Chapter 1

Leaving

"Leaving feels impossible. I cry into my suitcase where the cat sits, refusing to let me pack. He knows it's a bad idea."

The walls of my wooden home in Holts Field are thin. They were never meant to stand much winter and winters in Wales are cold, wet, and long. Each tiny change in temperature I feel in my bones. Each change in season I intuit first through skin. The house needs logs to feed the fire, which is its only source of heat. The water sometimes freezes in the taps. The toilet is outside, which throws me into surly wind, silent dark, early sky. All are metered with the regularity of an emptied bladder. I live partly outside, so the garden is my home, too. Daffodils along the willow hedge greet me each spring. A magnificent magnolia, standing guard at my back door, weeps white-pink flowers throughout the month of April. A broad elder protects me as I lie on the deck contemplating cloud-shapes in the blue of the sky. I have lived this way, raw and open to the elements, for twelve years by the time Australia looms. Leaving feels impossible. I cry into my suitcase where the cat sits, refusing to let me pack. He knows it's a bad idea.

Moving to Holts Field involved a steep learning curve, but from the time I first walked down the bumpy track and saw the little houses

HIRAETH

squeezed together around the outside of a muddy field, I was entranced. It was my first experience of living in this kind of close-knit community, but something in me was craving connection. I was a single, working mother. A creative type who loved having time to myself. Gregarious and energetic, my young son found school limiting and school, in turn, found him to be a challenge. Whereas he enjoyed lots of stimulation, I wanted less and in this way, Holts Field met both our needs. He got lots of playmates and a big, open space free from strangers, roads and fast-moving cars. I got my privacy, but with company and support available when I needed it. Over the coming years, despite being an only child, my son grew up within the warm bubble of security and belonging that comes with being part of a large family. Why would either of us ever want to leave? Well, as children do, my son became an adult and began to spend more and more time away from home. And me? I met someone.

Maybe I need to start thinking of myself in terms of a hero, setting forth on a great adventure. Or better still, a heroine. Writer and teacher Heather Jo Flores argues that while a hero begins with a desire, a heroine's journey begins differently :
"A heroine's journey starts with an inquiry - something she wants to know. She's curious. She has a question. A QUESTion. She wants to learn, to connect, and to transform. She wants to change the world." [3]

I can relate to that. One of the things I want to do in Australia is to make a film, which is not unusual for me. Film making, of one kind or another, has been my profession since graduating with a degree in Communication Studies in my early twenties. I worked alongside my photographer father, filming weddings and corporate videos, then spent some time in academia, teaching media studies and video production. It is whilst filming at Holts Field that I met Paul from Undercurrents, an alternative media charity using domestic video cameras as a tool in environmental activism. This new equipment not only made high quality images available at an affordable price, the cameras were lightweight and therefore more manageable for women. When an opportunity arises to open an Undercurrents workshop in Wales, I jump in with both feet. As well as activist videos, we deliver training and community arts projects, emphasising what I like to call positive alternatives. As a result of my media training, I am versed in concepts such as ideology. I understand how our world is shaped by social institutions like the family, school and church, not to mention the media itself. Increasingly aware of the social and environmental problems facing our world and of the tendency for minority interests (including women) to be silenced, I decide I want to be part of the solution.

Holts Field becomes more than a story, it becomes my home and the inspiration for a groundbreaking documentary project about low impact lifestyles and the value of community, optimistically entitled Living in the Future.
The ecovillages, intentional communities and co-housing projects documented by Living in the Future are indeed an attempt to change the world. They are, in a way, laboratories - an experiment in re-imagining the kind of community that was shattered way back when common land was enclosed and workers sent away to work in factories. These communities aim to live in harmony with the natural environment and to re-discover a way of life that serves the well-being of people.

When the Welsh government publishes guidelines for a radical new policy permitting sustainable development in the countryside, it is the first time since world war two that agricultural land is made available for development. The guidelines are stringent. Alongside co-founder Paul (Tao) Wimbush, Living in the Future documents plans to establish a One Planet settlement in Pembrokeshire called Lammas. [4] At a time when online video is scarce, the Media Channel in London sponsors a series of six internet programmes, but when the series ends, we realise there is so much more to say, so we simply keep going. To date, Living in the Future hosts over sixty short films and three feature documentaries.

These films are a record of a time in history which finds humans struggling to make sense of a world in chaos by learning from the past whilst utilising the technology of the future. Cosy, hand-built homes boast earthen walls and floors that hold heat and guard against cold. In place of concrete, structures are created from locally-sourced timber. Straw, sheep's wool and recycled newspaper provide an alternative to synthetic insulation. Fuelled by home-made compost, permaculture gardens overflow with organic, pesticide-free food.

Sometimes, the films make it all seem idyllic but we tried as well to convey the hardships, not least, in Wales anyway, the ever-present challenge of rain and mud. For those hardy folk undergoing these experiments, external challenges were more than matched with internal challenges. Giving up the comforts of modern life requires a robust commitment to both the philosophy and reality of what you are taking on, whilst the proximity of neighbours has always caused problems. At the premiere of our second feature documentary, entitled Lammas - How to Build an Ecovillage, I watch the film I have directed, shot and edited as if with fresh eyes. The audience enjoy the story. They laugh in the right places and clap at the end. The natural buildings look beautiful and the gardens enviable, but the understory is one of conflict.

Taking questions from the floor after the screening, I am left with my own burning queries. In addition to addressing the physical and practical challenges of our time, what inner tools do we, as humans, need to develop in order to survive? What does a truly sustainable life look and feel like? A week later, I pick up my suitcase and move across the world.

Chalet in Holts Field

Chapter 2

The Land Owns Me

"A crowd has gathered to bear witness, summoned by a phone tree which alerted five people, who each called five."

The Wales I love is green and blue. Gray at the mountains and cliffs, yellow at the sandy edges, but essentially green and blue. What makes it so green is the immense amount of rain and the blue, of course, is the sea that hugs our westerly and southerly sides. Though I appreciate the craggy heaps of the north and lush rolling hills of the mid, my devotion is kept for the sea sides. I grew up in Swansea, and my playground was the Gower Peninsula, Britain's first designated area of outstanding natural beauty. Here, the sea reaches twice daily across waiting sands in one of the world's longest tidal ranges. In the sea, my Dad teaches me to swim, holding me underneath my belly, encouraging me to extend my legs and kick my feet. In the salty cold waters of Horton, he introduces me to a lifetime passion, one we will share until his body is too frail to stand the cold.

They have sea in Australia, of course. If I take the number 96 tram, in forty minutes I can be in St Kilda. There, I can stroll along the promenade (like at home), drink an overpriced coffee in a busy beachfront cafe (like at home) or take a dip in the chilly, salty waters (like at home). It's so much like home, you'd think it would help assuage my homesickness, but instead, it just reminds me that I am not there.

Although I lived near the Gower all my life, spending childhood days clambering over rocks at Horton and adult afternoons wandering the cliff tops at Langland, the first time I walk the entire peninsular of Gower, it is to say goodbye. Facing two whole years away, I want to pay homage to this land that has given me so much. Beginning at my house in Caswell, I decide to walk around the coastline. My intention is clear. To make a pilgrimage to remind my homeland how much it means to me. To say thank you for the glorious camping weekends and the pre-Sunday-lunch hikes. For the before and after work swims and the evening beach barbecues. For always being there in its wildness. To make a plea that all will be kept safe until my return and most importantly, that my son will be kept safe. Honouring the sacred, I will weave spells and chant. Sing and maybe howl my prayers to the wind. Touch the earth and bury good luck charms in her precious body.

Taking only what I need, I stride away from my little chalet and across the field that holds the centre space of our small community. Camera. Spare battery. Flask, filled with hot water for tea. Swimming costume and sarong. Spare socks. Snacks - almonds and flapjack for energy. With my hiking boots hung from the outside of the pack, I tie a light windproof jacket around my waist and put on my sandals. A rare high pressure sits firmly over the peninsular and I've thrown out a call to friends who may like to join me, but I'm not disappointed when they don't come. This one is clearly for me alone.

The narrow walking track is unusually dry in this warm weather and my feet connect firmly as the path takes me down into the woods. I have walked this trail a thousand times. In the chill of dawn, as birdsong animates the canopy above me, mist rising eerily from the dense undergrowth. In the dead of night, feeling my way between trees as the forest closes thick darkness all around, owls hooting above my head. As a winter wonderland, snow cascading from the pink-gray sky, delicate silvery towers on slender, bare branches. In spring, bluebells forming their dense, bright carpet, my nose full of the scent of wild garlic. In Autumn, the smog of bonfires hanging in the dank, windless air. This path leads me to the sea. Over and over I have taken it. Over and over I have waded into the breath-stealing water. Over and over immersed my body in this natural temple. Over and over, felt blessed and renewed.

Today, at the start of my pilgrimage, my body feels heavier than usual. Both my pack and my heart weigh me down as I emerge from the woods and onto the friendly beach. Tall cliffs encircling the mouth of Caswell Bay, hugging me close. The tide is coming in and the morning swimmers gather at the top of the steps for their communal dip. I join in, wading into the shallows alongside them. This group swims every morning - on still, golden blue days of summer but also amongst the ice and snow of winter. Two of them, George and Prys, have been bathing here for over thirty years. Prys is a professor at the University and seems to know all there is to know about everything. George is an acclaimed local artist and between them, they have gathered quite a following. The old men lead the way, oblivious to the chill of the water, their skinny legs white as the stones glinting on the sea bed. Prys wears a red cap, tied tight under his chin like an Australian lifeguard. George's stomach protrudes over his bathers, his outy belly button giving him the air of a young child, in spite of his wrinkled knees. They waste no time, ducking their shoulders quickly under the smooth surface and setting about a brisk hundred strokes. Alun, a younger member of the group, swims out further, before turning and waving. When they start to retreat, I follow them up the empty beach to where their clothes hang neatly over the bench. A plastic washing up bowl is produced and into it, George pours warm water from a thermos before dunking his bloodless feet. As I tell them about my forthcoming adventure to Australia, they ooh and ahh politely, but they do not want to switch places.

One of the first connections I make in Melbourne is with CERES environment park. Inspired by the Centre for Alternative Technology in Wales [5], it is a potent mix of local produce market, fair trade cafe, organic plant nursery and bicycle repair workshop. There's a network of meeting rooms housing all manner of community groups, including, I'm happy to note, a yoga class and a meditation group. For someone with a passion for sustainability and community, who loves gardening, teaches yoga and has a steady meditation practice, it's a really good find. From my tiny apartment in Fitzroy, I can cycle there in half an hour, or I can take the 96 tram in the other direction, to East Brunswick. I've been in Melbourne less than a week when I first attend a class there and just over a month when the meditation teacher, Jess, says something which makes me sit up straight on my cushion. I even find myself leaning forward, my attention focused on her full lips. It's one of those times in a dharma talk when it feels as though the teacher is speaking directly to me.

At this point, a month into my life in a new country on the far side of the planet, I am feeling quite lost. During sleep, I find my way back to where the sand snuggles beneath my toes and the salty wind kisses my face. Come morning, as the light hits my retina, I am floored by the realisation that I am still here. Still not there. The pain that comes with this understanding sends a dense shudder through my belly. I miss the succulent land of my birth and am feeling stranded in this hot, urban intensity. What's more, there is a gap in my life. Where there was once family, friends and, perhaps most importantly for me, work, there is now a hole and it's big enough for me to fall through. A space has opened up. A wide expanse of nothingness. I'm spending my days fiddling with translations for the Lammas film or else wandering the streets of this strange city, daunted by glistening tower blocks and confounded by unfamiliar smells. I play housewife to Husband, who has walked straight into the safety of a job, with the comrades and HR support which accompany it. Cut loose in a city where I know no-one, I am floundering.

So when Jess starts talking about negotiating the feeling that we have a "space" in our lives, I am listening intently. The circle of people sitting on the floor around me disappears and only Jess and I exist. I watch her

THE LAND OWNS ME

hands, their gestures supporting her erudite explanations. Long, slender fingers. A silver ring with a dull red gemstone. I am pondering whether the ring is a significant one, when she catches my eye, bringing me back into the room. "When we feel we have too much space", she says, "it can be uncomfortable." "No kidding." I think. "We try to fill that space with something, anything. We call a friend, dive into work, or stuff down a muffin. We drown the emptiness in hot chocolate, or worse, in alcohol. Anything so that we don't have to face that void."

I recognise myself in her words. Facing the space means facing my sadness. The idea of opening myself to that void brings up fear, but even as she says it, there is some curiosity. In spite of my trepidation, I catch myself wondering what it's like to face the space. I tune back in to Jess.

"...but it's at the sharp edge of our discomfort that we learn the most. If we can just stay with it, what we'll find in that space is gold."

"Gold?" I think. "What gold?"

She tells a story about a girl, who is sent from her home in search of a magic elixir. The girl wanders far from her family, encounters and battles with witches and dragons, only to find that the magic she seeks needs to be forged within her own heart. I am thinking about the wizard of Oz and get caught in a musing about Dorothy and Toto before forcing my attention back to Jess. Now she's talking about a "point of reference" or "the safe place we go back to". When we are torn from what we know externally, this place, she says, is always available to us. It's our home inside.

Jess doesn't live in a community but as a teenager, spent two years living in a shack not dissimilar to my cabin in Holts Field. She refers to the experience as a time when she established a deep relationship both with herself and with the land. I don't get to talk to her about this until much later, but with this information, I already feel we share an important connection. There is something in a person's wide open, raw relationship with nature that gives them authenticity. Such people have a certain confidence in their own inner knowing and in the rhythms of life. I'm certain that when we live in sealed, airless boxes and move around in personal transport bubbles, we lose something important to maintaining aliveness. When we're too busy to take time to breathe deeply. When our food comes packed with artificial chemicals and disguised by cellophane. When communication with each other becomes defined by fear. In this kind of environment, we begin to lose our sense of humanity and with it, the ability to connect to life itself. Living closely with nature and with other people helps re-establish the connections that modern life severs, including the connection to ourselves.

When we choose our apartment in Melbourne, I like the way the floor-to-ceiling window faces the centre of the block. From my bed, I can see out to the green shared garden of Cairo. Built in art deco style, the tiny living spaces mimic the cabins of a cruise liner, their yellow doors inset with round port hole windows and long hand rails from which to lean and cooee your neighbour. The architect, Best Overend, designed this minimalist space for young men coming to the city from the country. [6] Overend was inspired by architect Wells Coates, whose Isekon building in London was called "an experiment in collective living for left-wing intellectuals". Amongst other artists of the time, the novelist Agatha Christie lived there and in its sleek, modernist lines you can see where Overhand got his ideas. Lying there, watching rays of sunlight filtering through trees and dappling the interior white wall, my mind reaches back to Holts Field, where my small chalet also faces the central common land. Shoulder to shoulder, our little wooden homes have withstood wind and weather since the 1930's, but Holts Field is far from modernist. In fact, it is a plot-land - a small parcel of countryside where folk from the city built cabins for weekends and holidays. During the second world war, those cabins served as sanctuary from the bombings and eventually, some people moved in as full-time residents. What's more, Holts Field has survived a twenty-year battle with the landlord, who bought the land for development and threatened occupants with eviction. On the winter day when the bailiffs finally arrive, I stand with my video camera, watching their ominous forms approaching. The caramel wisp of dawn has barely left the sky. The embers in the gatepost brazier glow weakly, its watch-folk gently slumbering. After months of careful preparation, the community is nevertheless caught off-guard. There is a scramble to secure locks and chains, but the bailiffs stride in anyway and demand possession. Startled children tremble amidst the noise and clatter. Muddy boots smear dark stains across swept carpets. Families are told to leave immediately, leaving dishes laid out for a breakfast that will never be eaten and last night's pots standing lonely in the sink.

A crowd has gathered to bear witness, summoned by a phone tree which alerted five people, who each called five. Using tactics brought from the activist movement, those five supporters called five more, until a hundred or so supporters stand in horror at the unfolding scene. When the warning went up, Joan rushed over to Karen's house, where she kept her promise to "lock on". Now she lies, her senior body bolstered by cushions, cheerfully holding one awkward arm inside a gap in the floorboards. Around her wrist, a handcuff is fastened to an empty gas bottle, which itself is shuttered into concrete. The bailiffs have sent for wire cutters, but the angle and depth of the hole makes it tricky, not to mention dangerous, to cut her loose. Neighbours bring tea for both Joan and the vicar who, in an act of bizarre but welcome solidarity, has chosen a bicycle D lock for his binding. All smiles, the two make headlines in the local paper that evening while the bailiffs, frustrated in this final task, are forced to abandon their mission. The sledgehammered door lies broken. A woman wipes her tears as her young son watches. What is so special about this place that it makes people defend it so vehemently? Why don't they just give up?

Tango in Barcelona

Chapter 3

The Things we do for Love

"Here is someone with whom I can wrestle the meaning out of life."

There's a pain inside and I'm trying to stay with it. My instinct is to drown it, eat it, yell it into oblivion but I'm crouching close, staying quiet, crawling inside it with an attitude that my meditation teacher, Jess, might call calm attention. I'm taking her advice. Turning towards, rather than away from. Looking closer instead of blotting it out. I don't think I'm afraid of what I will find, so why the desire to skip it? If it can't harm me, why move to change it? Why not sit with it and find out what it's about?

"How are you?". Every Melburnian asks me a version of that question. "How are you today?" "How's it going?" When I first arrive, I don't give an answer, not thinking that one is required. What could they really want to know? I learn, in time, to respond with something vaguely true. To pause, consider, say "okay" or "pretty good" or "not so bad, you?" With a real friend, I might elaborate. I might come back with "terrible" or "not as bad as last month" or "bloody awful, have you got two hours to listen"? Here, I haven't got any real friends, but I do have a meditation practice. What's my response when I sit on my cushion and ask myself how it's going? Do I give a flippant shrug or do I dare to answer truthfully, knowing that further investigation might cause even more discomfort?

When we meet, it is the way he sees me. The way he searches deep into the curly bits of my soul, making me blush. He is curly too. Chestnut brown ringlets reaching down over his collar. He is fearless. Unabashed. "Do you see the way he looks at you?" a friend asks. How could I miss it? He is in Edinburgh, the postcard says. He finds it thrilling to write to me. I read the card again, squeezing between the lines, into the loops of his letters, under the meaning of the simple words. Touched, I move towards him in my mind, telling my friend I am considering a date. Well, if he can be bothered to write...

We meet for a class - a private lesson with our teacher of Argentine tango. At the station, he holds a glass beaker containing a small white flower. Lifting it to my nose, I experience the intense, sensual scent of jasmine. I imagine him selecting the vessel from a row of possible containers in his lab. Clutching it as we walk through the warm streets, our words make a dance of their own - exploring wants, needs, opinions. Despite our difference in approach - our position at opposite ends of the arts-science continuum, the conversation slides quickly into deep places. There is something more to this than just attraction. Here is someone with whom I can wrestle the meaning out of life.

On a hot Sunday in July, he meets me again at the station, this time clutching a linden flower. At the beach, we lie side by side, touching from shoulder to knee, our hands deliberately grazing. We peek at each other through sideways eyes. We bathe in the grimy Barry sea, not touching in the water, but wanting to. We are in a group and yet completely alone, wrapped head to toe in possibility. On the way to the station, we stop at the funfair. The smell of grease and candy floss takes me back to childhood and I spin girlishly on the waltzers, still clutching the wilted flower. At every turn I see him, appearing and disappearing. The force of the spin throws me back against the red leather seats, a grin pinned to my face. A

THE THINGS WE DO FOR LOVE

giggle rises in my belly. Escapes my throat. The ride slows, the bar across my lap is lifted. My knees wobble as he helps me down the steps and so he holds me, one arm wrapped around my back until we reach the station platform. There, in front of everyone, he turns and kisses me and loving his audacity, I kiss him back, surrendering utterly to the moment. We take a seat a little away from the others and like teenagers, kiss all the way back to the city. When we get there, because we don't want to stop, we go to the cinema and kiss all the way through the film. We tango our way across the UK and up to Scotland, where he proposes. At the top of Arthur's seat, while I rest on the soft grass, he drops to his knee and produces a moonstone. "It's like you", he says, and though I'm still not quite sure what he meant, I like the analogy. Now, somehow, we have tangoed all the way to Australia.

I know when I promised to follow him. We were at his parents *dacha* in Belarus. We had travelled there for a holiday - first to Minsk and then a couple of hours outside the city to visit the allotment. It is like my hut in Wales, except with more vegetables. Neat rows of immaculate raised beds ripe with courgettes, aubergines and sweet, juicy tomatoes. Tall canes intertwined with beans make edible sculptures. At the bottom of the garden, an outhouse. It is then that I realise he is a peasant - a country boy. As a child he spent every summer with his grandparents in Ukraine and there, he helped work the farm, milking the cows and goats by hand and feeding chickens. Despite his civilised scientist demeanour, he has dirt under his fingernails. Relaxing in the dacha house that day, we curl up and talk about our future. I have only known him a short while but we always speak of the future. He wants to travel, he says. His work requires him to travel. I am done with travelling, I say. I travelled as a young woman. To Europe, the Caribbean, Egypt and South America. At thirty, I was ready to throw away my passport. I am happy where I am and the environmental movement supports my decision. Flying is bad for the planet. [7]
"But my work requires me to travel", he says, his voice urgent. He looks at

31 | 153

me, eliciting a promise which shakes me to my core and I nod, agreeing right then and there to go with him. My stomach flips over at the thought of leaving my little wooden home, my grown-up son, my cat, my community. Can I actually leave?

"Spain" he says. "I've always wanted to live in Spain." So he makes some applications and before long, we are taking a train to Paris. We dance in a little backstreet club before boarding the sleeper and rattling down through France to Barcelona. While he attends his job interview, I wander the streets, imagining what it would be like to live there. I visit Gaudi's home and walk through Park Guell and later, together, we take the cable car up to Montjuic. On a terrace above the city, we tango to the electronic beats of Gotan.

His interview is successful, but just as we are set to pack up and relocate, the funding for his post falls through. Europe is facing an economic crisis and there is no money left to employ him. One day soon after, I receive an email.

"How about that for a move?" he asks.

The link takes me to a job description outlining a post in Melbourne, Australia. How would I fare in a big city? I'm not sure, but if that's what life wants, I'm willing to give it a go.

"You've got two years", I say. "Then I'm coming home".

Hiking on Wilsons Prom

Chapter 4

Connecting the Dots

"Here on Wilsons Prom, they call the place Yiruk or Warnoon. Say it aloud and you will hear the land speak to you."

I've always been a bit of an edge-dweller and have spent many years watching from that vantage point. You might even say I've made a career of it. As a documentary film maker, I get to watch and listen from a safe-ish distance. But without my tools of camera and microphone, I often feel exposed. It's taken me years to feel comfortable in the Holts Field community and even now, I often shy away from social gatherings. It's true that I'm a natural introvert and there's nothing wrong with that, but is there also some fear? Perhaps of rejection or of not being liked? One of the most scary aspects of living close to others is that they might see the 'real' you. And yet, if I can face my own deepest vulnerabilities, might I discover something about the nature of conflict? Might I learn some secret to being in relationship, to being in community?

It's morning again. Opening one eye, tiptoeing into wakefulness, I can feel it's still there. That pain deep in my heart. I sigh. What will I do with it today? Will I gulp it down with cake, or obliterate it with strong dark coffee? Will I try to out-run it, out-cycle it or out-walk it -

HIRAETH

pumping my legs, my arms - making pain somewhere else so that I can no longer feel it in my soul? Will I work - making busy with plans and preparations, files and folders? Will I create a to-do list that will occupy me for weeks, months, years into the future? Today, I simply choose sleep. 'Just half an hour extra' I promise and then I get up, dress, drink some tea, write in my journal. I have a meeting and a lunch date. Both are disappointing anti-climaxes but they fill a few hours of my day with other people and I chat animatedly (too animatedly?) about the weather, the food, the economy. When lunch is over and I am alone again, I check. The pain is still there, like a worm or a mole, burrowing beneath the surface of my well-being. When I try to rise above it, I feel false - like too much make-up or an obvious hair piece. I laugh too loud, smile too widely, stare too deeply into people's eyes. I am seeking to connect, but all I see is my own discomfort, reflected in their gaze. In the lull of the afternoon I am confronted with loss. Loss of meaning, of fulfillment, of desire. Is this boredom? I take a tram to the beach, to see if it will make me feel better. A pair of young Chinese women pose on the beachfront, star-jumping for the camera. Is that what we do? Star jumps for our friends and our future selves, telling them that we're ok? I have no star jumps in me, so I sit and watch as a father runs side by side with his little daughter along the sand, letting her win the race.

How does one get to know a country? A people? Does familiarity arrive incrementally? Or does it one day tap your shoulder and announce itself, like a welcoming neighbour? At what point does one really arrive somewhere? For me, one such point of landing in Australia is our first visit to Wilson's Prom. Husband and I have studied the hikes in detail. How long they take and what the terrain is like. We choose a three-day option which takes us from Sealer's Cove up through the brushland and down along the beach to Waterloo Bay. The forecast for the weekend is hot. Very hot. In comparison to the twenty-odd degrees which blessed my Gower walk, this weekend is more likely to be forty. We question the wisdom of attempting such a long walk in such warm conditions but we've already booked our camp sites and besides, there are no wildfire warnings. With heavy backpacks and wide-brimmed hats we hit the trail, falling quickly into an easy silence. The heat softens my muscles and my hips feel comfortable as we negotiate the loops and twists of undulating paths. My mind softens too, thoughts swimming lazily in a relaxed pool of wide awareness. I watch the sway of my cotton skirt and enjoy the rhythmic contact of my sandals with the ground. It feels ancient, this way.

In a recent workshop, Aboriginal elder Aunty Carolyn Briggs told about her ancestors who frequented this area. The women of the Boon Wurrung clan were particularly skillful at catching seals, which are abundant on this stretch of coast and a rich source of food. To catch their prey, the women would frolic in the water with the animals, imitating their graceful movements. Once they had gained enough trust that the seals swam close, they would deliver a sharp blow to the nose, rendering the seal unconscious. History tells us that some of these canny native women were kidnapped by sealers and taken away from their homeland and today, descendants of these women, their blood now mixed with that of the white men who held them captive, survive as members of the Boon Wurrung clan. [8]

Aunty Carolyn has dedicated her life to fossicking for remnants of her ancestors' language and bringing it into everyday use again. When I tell her of my own heritage, she leans in, her face animated.

"So the Welsh have their own language?" she asks. I nod.

"When the English invaded Wales, they did the same thing as they did here. They tried to outlaw the Welsh language. But it survived."

"Can you speak Welsh?" she asks. "I'm not fluent" I respond, a lifetime's regret still hanging in my words. "But I learned it in school."

"Tell me some Welsh" urges Aunty, so I tell her how our *croeso* is her *wominjeka* and how we have a word that is untranslatable, but speaks of our yearning for *gwlad*, or Country. "*Hiraeth*", I say, the word catching in my throat. Aunty repeats it back to me, rolling the 'r' around her eloquent tongue. "*Hiraeth*".

At Wilson's Prom, I contemplate the First People as I walk. In the absence of our own voices, the only sounds we hear are the ones which have accompanied this landscape forever. Unrecognised birds call out from unfamiliar trees but their cries echo the feel of the place. I begin to understand how native things are named. In what little I have heard of the Aboriginal languages, words mimic the land. Speech burbles like streams, clicks like insects or rustles like vegetation. *Bundle bundle* is a form of grass found in the West; *Yorta Yorta* is a tribe in the South. Here on Wilson's Prom, they call the place *Yiruk* or *Warnoon*. Say it aloud and you will hear the land speak to you. Yiruk. Warnoon. Pronounce *yolla* over and over and you will hear the babble of the shearwater birds as they wake in their island home. Yolla yolla yolla yolla yolla yolla yolla. As my feet touch the earth and the land reminds me how to listen, I begin to arrive in this ancient country and find myself seeking out more opportunities to connect. I don't have to wait for long.

The Urban Coup are a group working to establish a co-housing project in Melbourne. [9] On this particular weekend, they are gathering at Commonground, an intentional community about an hour outside the city. [10] The property, which is also a facility for social justice activists, is tucked under the sheltering wing of the Strathbogie Ranges near a small town called Seymour. Commonground is home to a core group of about ten and refuge for a lot of visitors, from volunteers to woofers to social organisations like Urban Coup. Curious and excited to leave the city again, I accept the invitation. After my experience at Wilson's Prom, I'm not only looking forward to meeting new people, I'm looking forward to having new countryside to explore. As the car winds up Yellow Box Road, flanked by tall gum trees, we slow to negotiate the bumpy track and I wind down the window, letting in the sharp fizz of eucalyptus. In the near distance, sunlight catches a row of windows along an unusual, uneven building wedged into the hillside and I know that we have arrived. We step out of the car onto dry, stony ground, warm dust swirling around our feet. Inside

CONNECTING THE DOTS

the house, the contrasting cool air demonstrates appropriateness of design. Ruddy, contoured walls echo the muddy palms that caressed this building into being. It is so much like the natural buildings I have filmed, I feel I know this place already.

Caramel and ochre, umber and chestnut, muted colours create an impression that everything inside is simply an extension of the surrounding landscape. The high-ceilinged, open-plan lounge has a cosy nook where a nest of sofas curl around a wood fire hearth. The rest of the Urban Coup mob are already thumping through narrow corridors, bagging bunks in dorm rooms, rattling supplies into the kitchen and filling the huge urn for afternoon tea. I fill a mug and wander out to admire the view. A veggie garden with burgeoning greens and an apple orchard lead the eye down the hill towards a picturesque dam, while out over the tops of trees, a low-slung range of mountains shimmers in the distance.

With the kind of conversations flowing, I feel instantly among friends. I've been asked to make a short film about the group but I'm also here to enjoy myself. This place is so much like home. Fresh air, forest, the ability to walk out of the door and be in nature. And later, after a noisy dinner sat snugly around long, convivial tables, the familiar crackle of log fire and a wide canopy of stars in deeply dark sky. I sleep soundly and rise early the next morning to explore. Finding a sheltered spot, I sit quietly with my camera, recording ecstatic sounds of daybreak in the Australian bush. Kookaburras call out hilariously. Magpies tootle tunefully. From the undergrowth, a kangaroo lopes. As she ambles along, nibbling tussocks of coarse grass, a joey leans out of her pouch to reach for his own breakfast. I shift a little to turn my lens toward them and she lifts her head, ears twitching like radars. She shrugs, brings one huge back paw up to scratch her haunch and lollops off.

The Urban Coup crew spend the weekend planning a design for their buildings. They have their eye on a piece of land in the north of the city

HIRAETH

and have brought in an architect with experience of co-housing to help them through the process. The hand-crafted mud brick and timber framed buildings are perfectly suited for workshops, with plenty of light-filled spaces inside and out. A professionally-equipped kitchen hums with joyful activity as volunteer cooks create vibrant, wholesome meals. These weekends away have helped the people in this project build a sense of community long before they attempt to live together. They are learning about how to make decisions, how to work as a team. Important as they are, it is not all about the buildings. It's about respect, consideration and good communication. It's about friendship and maybe even love.

"I think a lot of us have a sense that we've lost a sense of neighbourhood." says Sally, a founder member of Urban Coup. "And when it came to the brass tacks of owning a house, I knew that I couldn't afford to have a big house with a vegetable garden and all the things that I would want. But I also didn't want to live in a little apartment, locked away from everything and without the ability to grow food and be connected to the land. So to me, this is the best of both worlds. I get to have my little apartment with my own little space, but I also get to have a community around me and all the things that we can share in terms of sustainable infrastructure."

Commonground itself was developed much in the same way. Years before they got this property away from the city, a group of friends who worked in the field of social action had a vision. They experimented first with a share house in the suburbs, spending time gathering skills, information and resources. Eventually, they acquired this land with the clear intention to create a resource for those working for social change. It was to be a place where groups could meet and plan, just as The Urban Coup are doing now. That was the early eighties. Underpinned by socialist and feminist principles, they shared everything, from building and household tasks to childcare and income. "One roof, one purse" was how they described it, though they wisely insisted that each individual had their own room - a practice that survives to this day and which they claim has saved both friendships and marriages.

CONNECTING THE DOTS

"People always asked if we shared partners too", says Kate, one of the founding members. The answer is no, we didn't, but we pretty much shared everything else!" In sharing their space and their vision, as well as skills in communication and group work, the team at Commonground have helped many other communities develop and grow, including Moora Moora, Melbourne's other well-known, long-term intentional community. [11]
While Commonground is turning thirty, Moora Moora is celebrating its fortieth year. To get there, I need to catch a train and a bus. Even then, I won't be able to reach Moora Moora until someone comes and picks me up from the nearest village. My train takes an hour just to leave urban sprawl and it's not until I'm on the bus that we reach trees. The landscape turns abruptly from grey to green. Square, hedged fields play host to large, ranch-like properties. Tall clumps of gum trees stretch graceful limbs into a wide sky. Something in me breathes out.

Sandra is waiting at the bus stop. She wrestles a huge armful of weekend papers into the back of the car and turns to give me a hug.
"So good to meet you!" she cries and I get the feeling she really means it.
From the village, we take a road winding upwards. On either side of the car, dense forest closes in and there is a sense of ascending into clouds. Through the window I see nothing but thick tree trunks carrying the eye skywards. Sandra drives the narrow road with the air of one who knows it well. I have read that she is one of the founder members of Moora Moora, so I ask her how she and Peter, her husband, came to form this group atop Mount Toolebewong.
"In the twenties and thirties, the land was used as a holiday destination for people from the city." she says, her eyes not straying from the road.
"Their lodge house is our community centre where we hold our meetings and communal meals. From the lodge, we built out on each side, in clusters of five or six houses. There are about twenty homes in all."
We've pulled out of the main road through a gateway, where a grassed area splits the path in two directions. "We'll head for the cafe first. Would

41 | 153

you like a cuppa?"

On a children's blackboard, a hand-drawn cup and saucer welcomes us to the community cafe. As Sandra opens the door, a rush of chatter sweeps out and she ushers me inside, pulling the door behind us against chilly mountain air. The room is half-full of people, who all glance up as we come in. Behind a counter, a woman stirs a vast pot on the stove from which rises the steamy scent of cardamom. "Chai" announces a folded piece of card on the counter top.

Sandra introduces me to a few people and I find myself immediately enjoying the warmth of attention as people turn their chairs and start to quiz me.

"Where am I from? How long have I been in Australia? What's the film I'm making? Where else have I been?"

I answer them as best I can until I spot Sandra gesturing over their heads. I snake through to the counter and order a chai and a hot apple muffin, paying a fraction of what I would fork out in Melbourne. Negotiating my way back through the chairs, past the table where Sandra has laid out the papers, I'm surprised to notice The Australian there as well as The Age. I suppose I expected communities like this to be full of left-wingers but in reality, there's a strong conservative element to this kind of life. I wonder how they manage to reconcile those political differences and as if in response, the conversation starts to get a little heated at the other end of the table. Peter is leaning in and waving a finger in the air to make his point.

"Don't take any notice of them" says Sandra, following my gaze. "They're old duellers."

The memory of lively exchanges around the communal table back at Holts Field makes me smile. Differences of opinion are not always a bad thing. They make life interesting.

Sandra explains how the community functions, her clear, blue eyes

CONNECTING THE DOTS

fixing mine as she speaks. It helps me focus on what she is saying above the din.

"There are five 'clusters' of houses, each with some autonomy within the group whole."

Sandra makes little circles with her hands to illustrate her point.

"We did a lot of research into how communities worked and decided this was a good way to help safeguard against total disfunction."

I take a bite of the muffin, licking sugar from my top lip.

"If one 'cluster' is not doing so well," continues Sandra, "the others can usually pick up the slack in terms of cohesion. It works, mostly."

I imagine our huts at home, nestled in close to one another, our boundaries marked by low hedges or a wooden fence.

"What are things that would make it 'not do so well?' I ask.

"Oh, conflict, usually. People not getting on. Or just generally having a hard time of it. It takes a lot of energy to live in community and sometimes your own personal life takes it all up."

Compared to Commonground's ten members, Moora Moora has nearer forty. That's still small enough to know everyone's names and big enough for there to be people you can avoid. Sandra emphasises the importance of communal work days, when people get together on a shared project. It might be gardening or building, painting or chopping wood. For each work day, a team from one of the clusters will cook for everyone.

"Food. That's a really important bit." says Sandra, chuckling again.

Before they set up Moora Moora, Sandra and Peter lived in a few other communities. Peter was carrying out research for his PhD and wanted to get some real life experience. One of his conclusions is that there is a continuum of sharing - from communes, where people share everything, to private homes, which share nothing.

"Intentional communities", he says, "negotiate public and private space. What is not designated to be shared, is assumed to be private. Boundaries are really important so that everyone knows what they can and can't do."

Boundaries exist at home in Holts Field, but in a more casual way. There is no organised leadership, not even a committee. When the community needed to mobilise against evictions there were meetings but, since then, communication is by word of mouth or occasionally a note through the door. More recently, residents communicate via a private Facebook group. It's by no means perfect. Sometimes 'politics' between people drag on and there's the odd explosion when someone oversteps what is considered to be a commonly-held 'norm'. There are spats over rubbish and car parking but these are just part of the daily living-next-door-ness. Animosities tend to fizzle out naturally. One of the things that people seem to dislike most about the idea of intentional communities is endless meetings. In Holts Field, if people want to do something, they self-organise and do it. If nobody wants to do it, it doesn't get done. Having said that, there will always be some who take more responsibility than others. Is it any different anywhere?

Commonground Community, Victoria

Chapter 5

Not the End of Suburbia

"We really aim to put what is in the best interest of the community ahead of our personal interest."

My breath feels as though it's stuck in my chest. I'm pushing it out deliberately, using the muscles in my stomach to force an exhale but it rushes back in and lodges at the top of my lungs. This leaves me with a sense of anxiety, of something about to happen. It's exhausting. I've taken to walking round and round Carlton Gardens, the park opposite our Cairo apartment. It helps a bit. It's not exactly the wild of Caswell beach, but there are mature trees, flowering shrubs and a large expanse of grass on which to laze, or lay out a mat and do some yoga. Mostly, I just walk. The route varies, sometimes taking me up alongside the Rubik's cube wall of Melbourne Museum, sometimes down past the children's playground. There's always something going on to help distract me, or to help me connect with other people. Lately, a group of Chinese women have been performing an exercise routine every morning on the basketball court. Lining up behind each other, they march and sway and stretch in unison to recorded Chinese music playing from a beat box in the centre of the court. All the time they are moving, the women are smiling. To themselves, to each other and to passers by who gaze with amusement at this cultural display. Like these women, my time in the park punctuates my day and I'm coming to love the quirky nuances of life in a multicultural city. I still ache for the wildness of Gower but while there is less potential for nature connection here, there is more potential for human connection.

When we were scouring the internet for places to live in Melbourne, we stumbled across Murundaka co-housing project. [12] It looked interesting, not only as something with story potential, but as a nice place to live. It has eleven apartments, one, two and three bedroomed and a large community space with shared kitchen and laundry. I liked the idea of it, especially as we knew no-one in Melbourne. It seemed like a quick way to make friends. But Murundaka is a long way from Husband's place of work, so we let it go. Until this point, most of the projects covered in Living in the Future have been in the countryside, but since coming to live here, I've become more interested in city-based solutions. After all, most people do live in cities, so we need to find ways to make it work better, both for people and for the environment. I'm curious about how co-housing works and, fortunately, the folk at Murundaka are very open to visitors.

At Heidelberg station, Iain Walker is waiting. He's tall and greying with a kind face and gentle eyes. Iain is a founder of the Earth Housing Co-op, which for the last thirty years has been providing secure, affordable housing for around a hundred people in this area of Melbourne. [13] When the two houses next door to one of their properties became available, they saw an opportunity to create something different. Although I've seen pictures online, when we pull up into the car parking area I'm surprised to see how big it is. Murundaka is a modern building, its steel and glass frontage softened by coloured 'welcome' flags over the entrance. In the common house, Iain introduces me to Giselle, a slim, dark-haired woman with palpable energy.
"I used to live here at this exact address, 42 Bamfield Road", says Giselle, pointing to the floor. "My house was basically a little farm and it got knocked down to make way for this. Now instead of three households on

this plot, we have twenty households involved in this community."

I look around the space, taking in big sofas, large tea urn and dresser lined with rows and rows of mugs. It's like a social centre but with the cosiness of a front room.

"I had a wonderful garden, with chooks and ducks. I raised my kids there. But the opportunity to build this was just too good to miss. We already have some glowing examples of community living in rural areas of Australia. Some very long term, well-established, wonderful communities. But we didn't have anything that was showing it in the suburbs. So for us to do the rapid transformative change that we need to see in our world, being able to do it in the suburbs was critically important."

Giselle takes me up to visit her sunny apartment. The living quarters are nestled around the central hub of the common house, with two or three apartments sharing a private balcony between them. Tables, chairs and well-tended pot plants indicate that these, too, are social areas. A cosy spot for immediate neighbours to share a cup of tea or glass of wine. It reminds me of the 'clusters' that Sandra talked about at Moora Moora, where the layout is designed so that smaller groups are formed within the whole. I can imagine there are times when a chat with your immediate neighbour is more personal, more spontaneous and perhaps less challenging than showing up in the common house. Inside her two bedroomed flat, colourful art covers the walls of Giselle's home and there is a feeling of warmth and stability.

"What is it about Murundaka that makes it different to a normal block of apartments?" I ask. Giselle is keen to supply the details.

"Murundaka is both a co-housing community and a housing co-op. We pushed for an affordable rental model, because we feel that security of tenure is empowering and enables you to get on with your life, without having to run around moving from one place to another all the time."

I nod, intrigued by what she is saying. In Britain, the system is set up so that the only way to stability and security is to buy your own home. But homes have become investments and house prices are increasingly out of reach for first-time buyers. What's more, the unstable nature of today's work culture makes a lifetime mortgage much more of a risk and the rental market is stacked in favour of landlords, who let their buildings on short-term leases. This uncertainty erodes community, as people are priced out of the areas where they grew up and have to move around to find work. Murundaka's affordable rental model aims to address all of these issues, but offers much more besides.

"Sharing is a key element of this kind of lifestyle" says Giselle, showing me the communal laundry, workshop and garden area. "It really is encouraging us to see ourselves not as separate individuals, living individualistic lives. The community entity that we're part of becomes an organism in its own right and the health of it, its well-being, becomes a dominant feature in the thinking. It's a bit of a struggle, but we really aim to put what is in the best interest of the community ahead of our personal interest."

This is no surprise, really. Amongst the intentional communities that survive longest are those that feel they serve a wider purpose, such as religious communities. Participants are likely to have more shared values and principles, which is personally validating and probably causes less friction. I wonder if we can all benefit from a sense of not living only for our own small self? Having a shared sense of purpose increases our sense of belonging and this surely applies to neighbourhood projects, like-minded groups and all sorts of action or hobby-based gatherings. Could strengthening our connections with each other be simpler than we think?

I ask Giselle how they deal with conflict and she gives me a wry smile and takes a deliberate breath. "Initially you just see the subject matter. The trigger. Food, for instance, is one that is contentious the world over, in all communities, at some point in time. Also participation, even just in terms of turning up to community meals. When people aren't engaging in the social side of the community enough, you don't get to know them and the natural conversations don't happen. The communication gaps start to widen. The opportunity for assuming, making judgements and getting it wrong, start

NOT THE END OF SUBURBIA

to really increase and it's a deterioration. An unravelling. So getting people together is really vital. But the thing then is how to resolve the conflicts."

I find myself wondering about what we do at Holts Field when there are squabbles. In particular, I remember a conflict I had with one of my neighbours. I didn't handle it too well. In truth, I'm pretty terrible at dealing with arguments. My tendency is to go quiet and withdraw. Here is an opportunity to explore my own shortcomings under the guise of more research. Am I brave enough to take on that challenge?

"At Murundaka, we are drawing on the expertise of other communities and the wisdom that exists there, but we have to practise these things and we are learning. We have a community mediator and we've been learning how to do mindful communications. They help us then have the conversations in a more constructive way."
Mindful communication? I can see that I'm going to need some more help if I am to learn more about how to deal with conflict.

Whilst being aware that mainstream Australia has inherited many of these unhelpful housing, economic and social models from Britain, there is one additional conflict that runs through the whole of Australian society. Murundaka, meaning 'home' or 'place', is a word from the Aboriginal language indigenous to this region. Like Sandra and Peter at Moora Moora, the founders of Murundaka requested permission from local elders to use the word and in doing so, acknowledged the traditional ownership of the land. I, too want to find a way to acknowledge Aboriginal people in my film, but when I ask a white arts professional if I can approach an Aboriginal elder for an interview, she says no, it won't work that way. To illustrate how 'blackfella' protocol might work, she offers a story from a time when Aboriginal people roamed the continent in different tribes. For instance, when someone from a neighbouring tribe wanted to make contact, he would set up camp at a distance, close enough so the elders could see his fire, but not so close as to constitute a threat.

51 | 153

Having established his presence, the seeker would wait - sometimes for days, sometimes months, until the tribe was ready to invite him to make connection. Then a messenger would be sent to invite him in. In order to reach out to Aboriginal people, I figure I have to set up my camp and make my presence known, but I have to confess that I'm concerned about how long I may have to wait. I think about what Giselle said about taking the long view, and it occurs to me how bad we Westerners are at that. We want things done today, or even better, yesterday! Still, my intention remains, so I take myself off to do some research at the State Library of Victoria, only a ten minute walk from my apartment.

The beautiful high-domed State Library building has an air of culture and seriousness. In the reference section, I select a small pile of relevant books and settle into seats of dark wood and green leather. *Terra nullius.* The legal term the British used to claim, in spite of well-documented evidence to the contrary, that when they arrived, the land of Australia was unoccupied. Lengthy, disturbing accounts of mass murder and torture. Whilst history is clear that this happened, it was airbrushed out of the school syllabus and it took a full two hundred years for a case involving Aboriginal land rights to be brought to court. I find evidence of a case - Mabo vs Queensland - where the land rights of the Meriam people, traditional owners of the Murray Islands in the Torres Strait, were finally recognised. The Mabo Case challenged the existing Australian legal system and on 3 June 1992, after more than six years in the courts, six out of seven High Court judges upheld the claim and ruled that the lands of Australia were not in fact terra nullius or 'land belonging to no-one' when the Europeans arrived. They also ruled that the Meriam people were 'entitled as against the whole world to possession, occupation, use and enjoyment of (most of) the lands of the Murray Islands'. [14]

The High Court recognised that Indigenous peoples had lived in Australia for tens of thousands of years and enjoyed rights to their land according to their own laws and customs. They had been dispossessed of their lands piece by piece as the colony grew and that very dispossession enabled the development of Australia as a nation. Ultimately, the Native Title Act was inserted into Australian law, making it possible for other tribes to make claims. I wasn't yet sure how this information would feature in my story, but knowing and naming it seemed important. Despite there being no word for it in their traditional languages, Aboriginal people are now six times more likely to commit suicide. Generational trauma explains many of the symptoms of depression and anxiety which can lead to such cases, but so too can the simple fact of dispossession from the land. In losing connection to their land and their communities, Aboriginal people lost too their ability to connect to their own inner life. If they were Welsh, we might call that *hiraeth*.

Dharmananda, Northern New South Wales

Chapter 6

A Home Economy

"The place of the woman in the home has been badly maligned. To take away the value of the household economy is very sad.""

The first signs of Spring are unfolding and a warm evening blows the sticky scent of jasmine in through my open door. All of a sudden, I feel a rush of love for Melbourne. I step outside onto the balcony, basking in the warm glow of lights from my neighbours' homes. Despite being right in the middle of the city, I feel safe. If I cried out, someone would help me. Is this what home means? Feeling safe? The horseshoe formation of the building hugs me close and I realise once more how similar this feels to Holts Field. How the living spaces are near to each other, yet maintain their privacy. How the sounds and the people are familiar. The front gate slams and Karen emerges from the shadows. I hear her key find the lock and watch the light from inside her flat spread yellow over the garden. The light withdraws and she disappears, closing the door with a click. In the book I am reading, local author Maya Ward walks the length of Melbourne's Yarra river from mouth to source. She relates a magical journey, entwining personal experience with history, myth and legend. She labels it a pilgrimage, which inspires me to adopt a mystical stance to my upcoming trip north.

Driving from Brisbane Airport deeper into Queensland, I stop to get my bearings. A whooping and whistling rises from the trees, like an old pal running to greet me. Crystal Waters has a very distinct sound, which I used to begin Ecovillage Pioneers, the first of Living in the Future's ecovillage films. I'm happy to be back, but Crystal Waters does not seem happy to see me. Looping up through the village in my bright orange 'Spaceship' rental, I get stuck in a dead end. A sharp-faced woman with a wagging finger frowns through my window.

"What are you doing sticky-beaking round here?" she demands.

I explain who I have come to visit and she seems to let me off but later, I am told that people here can be less than welcoming to strangers because "they value their privacy."

That night, I wake with a start. At first, I think I am in my bed in Melbourne. Then, disoriented, I don't know where I am. It comes to me that I have two homes, one in Wales and one in Melbourne, although more and more, it is Melbourne that is my habit. I ponder this, putting off the moment when I will have to climb out of my warm nest and venture out to pee. Outside, stars litter the sky and a crescent moon hangs low. I whisper an offering to this beautiful land. In the distance, something howls and from next door, I hear the growling and screeching of possums. Whoever said the countryside was quiet?

When I was last here, I interviewed Morag Gamble. She and her husband Evan are founding members of Crystal Waters and are world-renowned permaculture teachers. In the edit suite, I watched her beautiful face a hundred times, long blond hair falling around her shoulders, telling me how permaculture is not a dogma but is a way of "observing the patterns in nature, observing the patterns in our culture." It is ten years since I was last here and Morag has had two children in that time. I feel like we are old friends but this time, I am here to see Robin Clayfield, who is running a course in what she calls 'social permaculture'. [15]

I hang back and watch for a while as Robin leads the participants in some exercises before getting our my camera and starting to film. Sitting in

A HOME ECONOMY

circle, focusing games, weaving a spiral hug. The workshop is designed to create closeness and a sense of equality.

"This is the art of group work" Robin explains.

Recalling my 'sticky-beak' encounter, I wonder out loud whether her practices work in this community.

"Some people are into it." she shrugs, with an air of acceptance. Acceptance is one of the qualities Robin values most highly in community.

"There are 250 of us here, including all the kids. I've learned to say 'well, that's so-and-so, and I love them, but I don't always agree with them.'"

There's a fair amount of disagreement hereabouts. Over dinner, a group of residents chatter about people "having a go" at each other over the internet. One of the members had 100 emails today from a disgruntled thread! If Robin's techniques offer a better way to communicate than stroppy emails, I want to learn about them. When I drop by the common house the following day, she is taking a break from the course and I grab her for a one-to-one interview.

"I work a lot with dynamic decision making techniques." she says.

"Helping groups have discussions so there is not so much need for problem-solving and conflict resolution. The more we connect and know each other personally, the more likely we are to get through the hard times."

That's almost word for word what Giselle said to me at Murundaka. Getting to know each other seems like an indispensable tool when working with conflict.

"One of the things that we don't do here that I see works really well in other communities, is eating meals together. I've watched communities like Earthsong in Auckland, New Zealand share meals very regularly. Those communities are much more bonded. Much closer than we are here."

What I'm hearing is that here's something about regular social connection and doing stuff together that helps create community. It doesn't seem like rocket science, does it? But so much of our public life has become a spectacle. We watch other people doing things, rather than getting involved. A lot of the time, we watch them on TV from the safety of our own front rooms. Even the cinema, which used to be a quite a collective activity, has been turned into an orgy of consumerism. Robin says that maintaining that focused connection is more possible in smaller communities but even many families don't take the time to eat together. Could this recipe for harmonious relationships include something as simple as sharing food?

After the shaky start, I'm beginning to enjoy my stay at Crystal Waters. I accept an invitation to their Saturday market, where one of the residents has set up a sourdough bakery and coffee shop. People sit around and chat like in any local square and it's obvious there is a lot of love here. But my schedule demands I move on to the next place, the next living experiment and the next interview, so I take my leave, pointing my Spaceship north.

Over the border in New South Wales, Lismore city council refer to Dharmananda as a 'high-functioning community'. This gives an indication of its status in the 'Rainbow Region', where intentional communities grow like (magic) mushrooms. When I arrive, I am invited to join their shared supper, prepared by members of the community with produce from their own small farm. Sharing food they have grown together? I'm expecting this community to function really well!

I am here to talk to Carol Perry, whom I know from Melbourne as one of the people who teach alongside Jess at CERES. Those who expect her diminutive frame to signal a fragile person, don't be fooled! Carol has finely-tuned insight and razor-sharp wit. In fact, she confides that she once dabbled in stand-up comedy, though I can't persuade her to treat us to a performance. She is one of the founding members of Dharmananda and is regarded an expert in conflict resolution, but it wasn't always so.

"When we came here we were dreadfully naive", she explains, her gray-blue eyes twinkling mischievously beneath short, neat hair. "We had no way of knowing what to do when things went wrong. And they did go wrong." Despite it being the early eighties, and despite there being a dearth of courses in group work, Carol managed to get some training and found that

A HOME ECONOMY

she had an aptitude. "I was good at it." she says simply.

At Dharmananda, she has helped to put a number of guidelines in place. For instance, there is an understanding that if a community member has an issue with another member, that member may discuss that issue with someone else only once. After that, it is time to address those feelings directly to the person with whom they have the problem. It's easy to see how this avoids a complaint becoming either whinging or gossip. Carol explains that although many of the community practice meditation, it is 'skilful means' that are most highly prized.

"If I can distill the dharma into one thing" she tells me, "it is 'in which direction are you looking?'

It's this way" she emphasises, jabbing a finger at her own chest. "It's this direction."

This policy of personal responsibility extends to work areas, too. Picture this. Broad-brimmed hats bent low against the climbing sun. Neat rows of leafy greens being tended by hand in focused huddles of activity. A huge cauliflower plucked and brandished proudly for my camera. Saturday mornings are community work time and everyone comes together to tend to the farm.

"Each resident takes responsibility for a certain vegetable." says Carol, wandering between the furrows. "That way, if the vegetable is not doing well, it simply doesn't appear on the table. And we know who to ask why." Since everyone only cooks once a week, community meals are a feast. Sitting down to multi-coloured dishes of vegetables, grains and pulses, the Dharmananda appreciation chant sounds out, rising into the air in the way a group of yogis might chant the OM. "YUUUUUUM!" And it is, too.

Through the morning mist, I can make out Leigh's red sweater as he chivvies the cows along the valley. None of them seem to be in a hurry, except perhaps the young calf, who dances about, racing ahead and then turning playfully and bounding back. They take little encouragement to

HIRAETH

file into the milking stalls, bowing their big heads into the feed buckets. Leigh draws up a stool. He milks by hand, tugging at the leathery udders, sloshing steaming liquid into a steel pail. It's still early when he carries the full buckets up the steep steps to the communal house, where fellow community member Maggie is waiting. A huge vat sits on a burner on the kitchen floor and into it, Maggie pours the fresh milk.
"Have a seat" she invites. "This will take a while".

Maggie adds rennet and sets a timer, then unwraps a round of cheese and hands me a slice.
"This is what we're making", she says. The pride is evident in her face as she watches me enjoy the crumbly sharp creaminess. Satisfied that she has proven the value in what we are doing, she steps back to the vat and takes a long flat blade, drawing it smoothly through the congealing milk.
"This is called cheddaring" she explains. "Because we're making cheddar!". While she works, I tune my ears to the steely, rhythmic tapping. In that moment, it seems that Maggie is enacting a scene from an old nursery rhyme. She is Little Miss Muffet, practicing the ancient skills that were once part of everyday life.

Curd slops like scrambled egg into the waiting cheesecloth bag. Living in a world far removed from its original use, cheesecloth has to me always meant ruffled gypsy blouses, but Maggie hangs it from a kitchen door handle and kicks a bucket underneath to catch the whey. Down beneath the house in the cool of the cellar, Maggie shows me rows of cheeses stacked up in the fridge, and a handwritten log that records who has turned the cheese and when. Each log notes the weather at the time the cheese is turned, so that a complete picture of the life of the cheese emerges and once again, the responsibility for success - and failure - is spread throughout the community.
At 11am people appear, stepping out of muddy boots into warm slippers. Moist carrot cake is laid out alongside a plate of crusty warm bread. A pot of lemon curd with home-printed label sits next to a small, hand-carved

wooden spoon. A bowl of salad is dressed brightly in orange nasturtium flowers. Everyone dives in, helping themselves and serving each other and the house lights up with chatter. Morning tea in Australia is a ritual they think they have acquired from the old country, but in the old country now, you are lucky if you get a ginger biscuit with your cuppa! It brings to mind my grandmother, who took 'elevenses' and always had home made cake or biscuits set aside for visitors. In summer, she replaced tea with a refreshing glass of home-made elderflower champagne. She would have approved of the many spendthrift ways of creating abundance that are a part of modern eco-communities.

The Dharmananda community is eighty-five percent self-sufficient in food, a figure which reminds me of the terms by which the Lammas ecovillage in Wales obtained their planning permission. In return for a licence to build natural homes in open countryside, they committed to obtain seventy-five percent of their needs from the land. This meant not only growing their own food but also using timber from the community-managed forest for building and fuel; weaving baskets from willow; harvesting honey from bees; creating a business from foraging; making cosmetics from flowers or turning wood for plates and furniture. In the seventies back-to-the-land movement, this was called self-sufficiency. Now, in the post-carbon economy, it's called resilience. The terminology has a tendency to ignore the inter-dependency of smallholdings but the economics model created by lifestyles like this is dependent on something we might call a shared economy. Even more than this, it is dependent upon a home economy.

Home Economics in my school was a weekly double lesson when they showed us girls how to wash up (yes, really); how to shop; how to bake bread and scones; how to make staple dishes such as apple crumble and shepherd's pie. The ingredients were often those a housewife was advised to keep in her larder but in our family, they were more likely to be bought from the corner shop on the way to school. My Mum was a working Mum, one of the new generation that tended to buy stuff. Yes, she could bake, but it was easier and quicker for her to buy pies that Mr Kipling had made. With a full time job and two children, it's likely she didn't have much energy left for baking.

On the other hand my paternal grandmother, (we called her Nanan) was of a different generation. Family legend has it that she had never once bought a loaf of bread. She always baked her own. At Christmas time or on birthdays, we received recycled chocolate boxes full of sugary, misshapen, home made fudge, wrapped in paper re-used from last year and held together with an elastic band (so she could use it again next year). Nanan was really proud of her vegetable plot. When serving up a meal, she would sing that the potatoes were "from the garden!", tomatoes "from the garden!" or leeks "from the garden!". In Nanan's day, just one generation ago, housekeeping and the household economy was a serious job and she kept an accurate log of all household expenses. In his essay 'Money vs Fossil Energy: The battle for control of the world', permaculture co-originator David Holmgren writes about what happened to the home economy after the industrial revolution. [16]

"Women joined the workforce to help pay rising mortgage debts and support expanding personal consumption habits. The almost total collapse of the household economy followed. Much of the growth in fast food, home services, child care and entertainment industries simply reflected this shift of activity from non-monetary household self-reliance to the formal taxable economies dominated by corporations. Mounting psychosocial dysfunction expanded the need for the helping professions of health, social welfare and education as well as those of control from police and security services to deal with addiction, family violence and social fragmentation, both real and imagined."

David and his partner Su Dennett live on a smallholding in Hepburn Springs, a couple of hours from Melbourne. They exhibit a lifestyle deeply interconnected with the land on which they live and embody the basic principles of permaculture which espouse Earth Care, People Care and Fair

A HOME ECONOMY

Share. David spends quite a bit of time travelling to speak and teach, but Su is glad to make the home her place of work. She's welcomed me up to spend some time with her and in between tending the goats, the vegetable garden and the bee colony, she makes herself busy in the kitchen.

"I'm very happy to be the main cook and bottle washer and I think that the household arts have actually been maligned. The place of the woman in the home has also been very badly maligned. It's not that the woman should do this and nothing else, that's not the case, but to take away the value of the household economy is very sad."

Melbourne has fostered a strong hipster culture and as Su speaks, it strikes me that we might be grateful that hand-made things are becoming trendy again and that people are being encouraged to take up knitting, sewing, bottling and preserving. It's part of an older culture that knew the value of stuff and wasn't inclined towards waste. Upcycling is the new make-do-and-mend; rosti is the new leftovers and craft beer the new homebrew. My Dad, who grew up under the influence of Nanan's thrifty ways, would contentedly boast that his home-made beer cost two pence a pint. He might be shocked to learn that these cheap-to-make things have become of premium value, but of the home-made ethos he would definitely approve.

Perhaps the issue now facing those of us trying to imagine a world without an oil-based, cheap-electricity-driven, slave-labour-enabled global economy is how to upscale the lessons from these communities. Is it even possible to upscale without losing that essential connection to nature and to each other? How can our wider society enjoy a shared lifestyle which puts the well-being of the community first? The re-establishment of a home economy reduces our reliance on consumer items and increases our sense of interdependence. There is a real joy in making things. Meanwhile, at Dharmananda, Maggie's cheese-making workshops are becoming really popular!

Pool in Central Australia

Chapter 7

Conflict and Resolution

"Coming back to sensations in the body helps us ground, reorient, and then magically, to let go of the story and return to the present."

I'm watching my cotton trousers sway with the rhythm of my walk. The shadow of the sarong protecting my face moves sensuously over the gold and red ground beneath my feet. The day is winding down but animals are becoming active as the heat fades with the light. In the bushes, the odd rustle sends my heart beating and makes me quicken my step. We reach the swimming hole just as the sun dips down behind the rock face. The surface of the water is still, reflecting limpid blue from the evening sky. Tiny insects hover and dart about. The water is slippery-soft. My skin is so hot I half-expect to hear a sizzle as I submerge. We swim to the far end, where a waterfall rains into the deeper end of the pool. With day-warm rocks under our backsides, we join the miniature frogs basking in the cooling cascade.

The Aboriginal name for this place is Nitmuluk, perhaps from the *nitnit nitnit* sound of the cicadas now rising into the still evening air. Cicadas have long symbolised patience, inner knowing and timing, because they can wait up to ten years, underground or hidden in tree trunks, before choosing the right conditions in which to be born. Their sound is not, as I used to think, from them rubbing their wings like crickets, but is a toning from deep in their bellies. A hum to attract the right mate, so that they can make their short lives fruitful.

When the whitefellas came and settled here, they used the name Katherine for both the town and the river that runs through it. For over a hundred years, they occupied the area under that name before finally the local indigenous people won the right to make a claim. It took ten years for the claim to make its way through the courts, but when the land was finally returned to Aboriginal care in 1984, it resonated once more with the sound of its name. Nitmuluk.

This outback scene comes back to me whilst in a workshop on conflict resolution in Melbourne with Carol. As an exercise we are asked, within our groups, to remember an incident in which someone's words or actions provoked a difficult response in us. We each have to outline the event, tracking both our behaviour and the outcomes. I remember this...

On the way out of Nitmiluk, we take a wrong road. It's my fault. Husband is driving and I, the appointed navigator, am immersed in writing down my impressions and miss the turning, causing us to drive for an hour in the wrong direction. Husband is angry, which activates something painful in me. We'd both prefer some space from each other, but our insurance demands that we arrive before nightfall, so we climb back into the vehicle and keep going. Miles and miles of spectacular desert pass by. Ancient, bulbous boab trees. Blood-red rock faces. Nursing our own inner pain, bodies contracted and tight, frustration and a sense of wasted opportunity drains what little energy we have left. By the time we reach our destination, we are exhausted, both from the journey and from the effort of trying not to make the situation any worse. Over a solemn dinner, we try to patch it up, but some part of me has retreated, hurt, behind a door for which neither Husband nor I have the key.

Over a mango smoothie the next morning, I find myself softening.

CONFLICT AND RESOLUTION

Maybe I forgive myself. Maybe the psychological bruise just fades, but somehow, my armour melts away and I can once again feel love. Fortunately, Husband is more available too and we can plan the next stage of our trip.

At this point in Carol's workshop, we have to work out whether, in the playing out of our drama, we have been acting as 'persecutor', 'victim' or 'rescuer'. It's painful to watch ourselves as we take on each role in quick succession. Swapping and changing to try to get what we want.

"What's most important is whose fault it is." says Carol, that same old mischievous twinkle in her eye. And it's true, the instinct to apportion blame threads through all our stories as we struggle to get ourselves off the hook.

Carol asks for a volunteer and sets up a scenario at the front of the room, using the subject's own experience as an example. We watch, curious, as Carol shifts to face her 'client' and asks her to relate the relevant points in her story. Carol settles back and listens, nodding and encouraging, prompting the storyteller to re-focus when she strays from the point.

Watching her body language, we can all see when the woman feels grounded and empowered and also, at what point the details of her story have her caught in a 'state' beyond her own control. This is the essence of this training. To be able to feel in the body when a trigger event has crept up, surprised and trapped us. Held hostage by our own unconscious needs, we are as rabbits in the headlights, incapable of constructive response. We are slaves then, to wrong thinking, wrong acting, plummeting gracelessly in the direction we least want to go. Coming back to sensations in the body helps us ground, reorient ourselves, and then magically, to let go of the story and return to the present.

I still practice these techniques when I run into conflict or find myself triggered, and it helps that I can share them with Husband. When we meet difficult times in the future, we might laugh at our instinct to apportion blame and instead learn to address our own individual experiences. I'm not saying we never will get caught up in it, just that we have some tools to help to cut through the drama and set us free. With a willingness to drop personal armour, an ability to listen and an intention to serve the good of the whole, we are much less likely to spend ten hours crossing a magnificent desert landscape in angry silence.

Carol's neighbours at Dharmananda are Bodhi Farm, who also incorporated a commitment to meditation and conflict resolution when creating their community. One of their founding members, Stu Anderson, works with Aboriginal men's groups. He tells me about some of the techniques used for healing generational trauma in Aboriginal communities. It is during one of these conversations that I first hear the Aboriginal word *dadirri*, which Stu tells me can be translated as 'deep listening'. It refers to a way of being with the land, with oneself and also with other people.

"Practising *dadirri*", he says, "we tune in together. We sit with the land, with a person, with a problem, until we feel that the conflict feels completely resolved."

Stu admits ruefully that like many Aboriginal ways, this can take a loooong time. Back at home, I find a YouTube clip of an Aboriginal elder talking about dadirri. In a voice deep and deliciously warm, Miriam Ungunmerr-Baumann speaks as if from the edge of amusement, but her message is sincere.

"Dadirri is inner, deep listening and quiet, still awareness. Dadirri recognises the deep spring that is inside us. We call on it and it calls to us. This is the gift that Australia is thirsting for. It is something like what you call contemplation".

Deep Listening. Carol told us that we must offer this to ourselves. Ourselves first, and then others. She explained that when we offer it to ourselves, then there can be healing. We give ourselves what we most need - what we might think we need from others. Only then are we free to ask others what they need, because we can relate to them from a place of freedom, security and love. A friend of mine, who is also a film maker,

CONFLICT AND RESOLUTION

told me that when he is doing an interview and he's listening intently, his subject is likely to remain focused. What's more, unspoken questions pass between them and the interview has a magical flow to it. But when the interviewer is distracted by something - a flashing battery, or someone else coming into the space - the interviewee often loses the thread and forgets what she is saying. The energy of attention creates connection and holds a space for interviewer and interviewee to dive deep. Trust exists. Truths emerge. Could this kind of unconditional, non-judgmental listening be a key to resolving conflict?

JindiWorabak Dancers, Melbourne

Chapter 8

Always Was

"It's a bit like a patchwork quilt - the narrative of ancestors sewn into a piece of home-spun art."

I'm sitting peacefully in my apartment when I hear a hubbub in the street outside. Nicholson, the street on which we live, is a main artery through Melbourne, but today I don't hear traffic, I hear people. Lots of people. The rhythmic sound of their voices tells me it is a demonstration, so I grab my camera and rush outside. Traffic has been replaced by a river of black and brown faces.

"Always was, always will be, Aboriginal land!"

I follow the throng of people along Nicholson Street and past Parliament House. At the junction of Bourke and Swanston, the crowd pauses and forms a large circle. A man stands up and addresses the crowd.

"Our people have been walking this land for thousands of years. This place used to be a waterhole, before they came from England, before the concrete."

I imagine the land without the tall buildings, without the shop fronts, without the trams, the pedestrians, the buskers, the quirky sculptures of the three thin banker type men and the giant purse. Where Swanston Street runs down to Federation Square, instead runs a river, along the

HIRAETH

bank of which tall trees sway. And then, right there in the middle of the street, a fire is lit and an old man wearing a grubby bandana folds his legs nimbly beneath him and brings a didgeridoo to his lips. From the crowd, a dancer emerges, then another and another, all of them stamping a path around the musician. The dancers hold their arms out as if in flight; hopping and pausing, reaching to scratch a haunch or twitch an ear. They are kangaroos. They are birds. They are Bunjil, the Creator being, come to animate all life on earth.

I have arranged to meet my friend Pippa in the western suburbs of Footscray at an event which is part of the celebrations for NAIDOC week - the National Aborigines and Islanders Day Observance Committee. [17] Pippa and her partner recently showed the Lammas film in their solar-powered cinema at the Rainbow Serpent Festival. On the programme with me were an Aboriginal filmmaker called Robbie Bundle and his friend, well-known Melbourne elder and storyteller Uncle Larry Walsh. I'm looking forward to catching up with all of them again but at the last minute, Pippa has a family crisis and I'm left sitting on my own in the gallery, feeling much too white. I am rescued by Robbie, who greets me warmly with a "Hello stranger!", a welcome which moves me almost to tears.

The exhibition is like nothing I've seen before. On a white-painted plinth, a possum-skin cloak lies spread-eagled. The furry tails identify it as one of the cute squirrel-like creatures that scurry around the park after dusk, though the smooth hide could be any animal. The markings are a map. Wavy line denoting river. Spiral symbolising water-hole. The whole skin is a meaningful landscape or story. It's a bit like a patchwork quilt - the narrative of ancestors sewn into a piece of home-spun art. On the wall hang a series of photographs. Members of the same family wearing the possum-skin cloak. Against a stark white background, the faces of children, grandmothers and fathers peer out from inside the cloak. It curls around their heads like a hood, a shelter, a cave. The cloak offers the family something timeless. Belonging.

One of the family members is known as Uncle Roy. A portly, older man, his face has the ruddy complexion of a country farmer, his white hair escaping from under the hood. Until he was sixty-two years old, Uncle Roy believed what the mirror told him. He believed he was white. Then he learned that he had been taken from his Aboriginal mother as a boy and brought up in a mission, a victim of the stolen generation. In a sepia-coloured film, we follow a faceless woman through trees and grassland towards a river. Now and again, she beckons with one expressive brown hand and we almost catch a glimpse of who she is before she turns away again. For Uncle Roy, this is all he remembers of his ancestral tribe.

On an artist residency at the Pioneer Settlement in Swan Hill, I am making films with young people from rural Victoria. Along wide, wild west-style streets, a horse and cart carries tourists and school children and an early motor vehicle rumbles past old-style village shops. There is a bank, a printer, a draper and an ironmonger, but little recognition of the Aboriginal culture which the settlers displaced. In their mud brick houses, I see hints of the houses of the future - the ones built by people in the low impact communities I film. The contents, however, are remnants of the past. A huge wrought iron bed. A piano. A french dresser. All shipped from overseas to recreate a semblance of home comfort in this desert landscape. How hot those women must have been in their long skirts and buttoned-up blouses! How fervently they must have missed their homeland!

The schoolchildren I'm working with are descendants of these people. Some of their families have been in this area for generations. Their parents are farmers, growing grapes or oranges. Or they are teachers, doctors or business people. I work with them to create short narratives based on life in the Pioneer Settlement, and we shoot them on location in the dusty streets, our actors dressed up in fashions of the day. On the final night of the festival, we screen the finished films against the wall of the town gaol.

All these stories - those like Uncle Roy's and ones like the children tell, co-exist in this country. Stories of a people separated from their culture by force and stories of a people far from home, trying to make a new life. Were the white visitors acting out a trauma visited upon their own ancestors, who were pushed from the land to pave the way for industrialisation? The passage of traumas through generations was well understood by the ancients. In Sanskrit, the word *samskara*, for instance, describes the way impressions lodge in the body-mind, and is seen as both obstacle and entry point for healing. Perhaps the west's acknowledgement of how such patterns reverberate, whilst never excusing harmful behaviour, might open the doorway to fresh understanding.

In my motel room the following morning, I'm still contemplating the lineage we inherit from our ancestors when I receive a message from my cousin. My uncle has died.

Shanti Cat

Chapter 9

Dispossessed

"I can feel my ears resting into the deep quiet, released from the high alert of living in a city."

When I tell the taxi driver I'm from Wales, his response is surprise. "Well, I have just come from Australia", I confess. "That's it!", he says. "I thought I detected an Aussie twang". Sitting back against his comfortable leather seats, I wonder. Have I really been away that long?

In Cambridge, after a serene day of punting under a clear blue sky, me and my young cousins make Welsh cakes from the family recipe book. Written in the familiar hand of my late aunt, the recipes send a tentacle of remembering out into the past. Cheese straws. Fruit scones. My grandmother's recipe for elderflower champagne. This is the recipe I used year after year with the elder from my garden in Holts Field. The white powdery flowers bloom in late spring, so it was often warm as I sat on the deck and shook them into a bowl. Stirring in sugar and lemons, the scent of them filled my tiny house. During fermentation, the bottles occasionally exploded, sending a stream of sticky goo onto the kitchen walls, but it was always worth it. To taste again the sweet fizzy nectar of summer, inextricably linked to my resourceful female lineage, long after both summer and those women were gone.

"Where did she keep the flour?"

"In these old baby powder tins".

When I consider my current, rather rootless lifestyle, it makes me wonder for a moment who will bake Welsh cakes for my funeral. Will anybody know where I keep the flour?

Back in Swansea, my own mother and father rest at opposite ends of the same graveyard. Strange how this happened since, in life, they barely spoke after their divorce. Still, it makes it easy for me to visit them. I brush off my Mum's headstone, put fresh flowers in place and sit on the bench nearby.

"I'm back from Australia" I tell her. "Have I changed?"

Nothing.

"Are you proud of me?"

Mum stays silent.

I wonder if she has forgiven me yet for cutting her nails during that final stay in the hospital. Her bright, immaculately painted nails, stripped of their colour and poorly manicured by my amateur hands. I can hear those nails, tapping their accompaniment on the piano keys. I feel them scrape the back of my leg as she flips me. Cutting those nails off seemed like the final indignity. She slid quickly after that, her last breath long and easy, like a balloon relieved of its gas. A hollow wind through a one-way tunnel. I turn to my Dad. "Hey Dad." He shuffles a bit in my memory, as if getting comfy, but he says nothing to help my unease. I think back to his last breaths, taken in that same hospital building, almost five years after my Mum.

"There's a pattern" says my sister, watching his face intently. "Three breaths, then that little hiccup, see?"

I watch, but feel distracted by an intense itching in my legs. It's hard to sit still.

"Aye Aye" croons my sister. "Aye Aye" responds Dad, from somewhere deep inside himself.

DISPOSSESSED

This town, these streets, are so familiar and yet there seems no space for me. In truth, I feel more connected to my life in Australia. If I check my diary, all my appointments and commitments are there. It's been years since either Mum or Dad could offer me a home here and my sister, well, after Mum and Dad died, something seemed to break between us. When people ask me now if I have siblings, I have to confess that my sister and I are estranged. It pains me, but I don't know what to do except hope that, in time, our relationship will heal. Perhaps, with this exploration, I might learn the tools I need to help it happen.

I enjoy a few days in my chalet, kindly gifted to me by the current occupants. I delight in the sights, sounds and feelings associated with this little wooden home. I take the well-trodden path to the beach. Chat to my neighbours. I snooze with the cat curled on my lap. He's not forgotten me then! Sunlight makes a dappled appearance through the green. A light wind ruffles the ferns. Outside every window is green, from floor to sky. It's soft on my eyes and gradually, I feel myself relaxing, as though my whole being sits down. Released from the high alert of living in a city, I feel my ears resting into the deep quiet. At night, when the birds are sleeping, there is actually silence. No traffic, no-one talking, nothing. There is real darkness, too. No streetlights. No headlights. Just moonlight over the field and the gentle drip, drip of water through the trees. The creak of timber. The crackle of fire. A lone cicada chirruping in the bushes, like a visitor from that other place.

The cat is on his night shift. Hunting, no doubt. I sit on the porch as if to wait for him to return and realise that indeed, I am waiting for him to return. The house is lonely without him. Without my son. Without Husband. I recall the days when I liked nothing better than to have all of us under one roof. Me, Husband, my son and the cat. I could lie in the dark and feel the love in my heart wrap itself around our home like a comfort blanket. All of us here. All of us safe. Those were the

HIRAETH

moments when the phone ringing in the middle of the night was not scary. Everyone was here and everyone was safe. Will I ever feel such peace again?

I take my fears to my homeopath and she listens, her head tilted to one side. She asks questions, nods at my replies, hears my pain.
"You're dispossessed" she diagnoses. I roll the word around in my mind. "Dispossessed".
"I suppose I am" I agree. Naming the feeling helps. I am dispossessed, then. That's what this feeling is. My mind wanders towards all those people removed forcibly from their homes. Ousted from their land and moved to a place where they have no connections, no purpose, no history. Refugees. Asylum seekers. Migrants. Indigenous people. What is happening to me is a mere sip at the cup of dispossession. After all, I chose this.

Cairo Flats in Fitzroy, Melbourne

Chapter 10

Neighbours

"When people are isolated, they have to spend money to socialise."

I'm lying on my back in the yoga room at CERES, my eyes closed. Loretta's gentle voice lulls me into sinking deeper. "Take your attention to your right foot. To your right big toe, second toe, middle toe, little toe." Her pronunciation of "toe", like "toey" makes me smile. It's so Melbourne. Oops, she's already halfway up the right leg. My attention sways in and out until we reach the shoulders...and then "Gently open your eyes".

Where did I go? I'm sure I wasn't asleep. We are turning onto our right sides and remembering the intention we set at the beginning of the class. What was mine again? Oh yes, "My neck is comfortable and free from pain". No earth-shattering bodhisattva demands for world peace then. Just "free me from my own pain, please".

The yoga class leads into our group meditation session. I open the cupboard and begin to take the zabutons and cushions out and place them in a wide circle. A few of the regulars arrive to help. I take my place at the front of the room but my mind is still walking around, watching people enter and settle. I don't think I've really relaxed since I got back.

"Have you landed yet? " asks Loretta afterwards. "It takes a while, doesn't it?"

Yes, it does. During sleep, my dreams continue the busyness of my days. Last night, I organised a whole team of firemen to do a photoshoot as strippers. When I woke up, I was considering what kind of costume they would wear for the "beach" shots.

Husband takes me for breakfast before work. It's sunny and warm, so when he leaves, I sit for a while before I head back to my own desk. The café is fifteen minutes walk from our home and when I'm ready, I stroll back slowly through Carlton Gardens. A magpie flies overhead as if in slow motion, its black and white wings open to catch the breeze. A young couple stroll by with a dog, their take-away coffee in bright keep-cups. A city hipster strides past wearing a smart three-piece suit, briefcase tucked snugly under his arm. The green on the trees is diffused with gentle light and small, catkin-like seed pods wiggle in the breeze. It's so beautiful, I have to stop and sit again. I feel my buttocks on the park bench and ground my energy, breathing low into my belly. I don't want to rush back to work. I want to savour the spring morning. It occurs to me that in this whole, huge city, I want only to inhabit this bit. Right now, this little bit is enough. The thought comforts me.

Our neighbour, Michael, calls himself a Fitzroy boy. He lives in Fitzroy, works in Fitzroy, plays in Fitzroy. I appreciate the simplicity of his life. In Michael's work as an architect, he is an advocate for minimalist living. He renovated his twenty-four square metre apartment so that he has everything he needs to be comfortable. He took the visionary Cairo style bequeathed by the architect Best Overend and made it more adaptable, with a pull-down bed and a full wall of storage space hidden by a glamorous, sweeping curtain. After he did a similar makeover for one of the neighbouring apartments, he gained the nickname 'Second Best', a homage which delights him. Michael regularly brings architecture students to visit the Cairo building and every year, he acts as tour guide for Melbourne's Open House initiative. For him, Cairo is a model for a better quality of life in the inner city, a model that seems to be on trend. The Tiny House

NEIGHBOURS

movement echoes the minimalist theme of Cairo even with Australians, who, Michael says, love their big homes. [18]

"I've always enjoyed living in small places with minimal things" he tells me. "I don't really enjoy the burden of a large house, or the responsibility of it. I don't want to spend my life looking after a place and cleaning a place. Essentially you just become a custodian of a house, rather than living a life."

My neighbour on the other side, Mitra, also loves living at Cairo. A friend of hers insists that if Mitra wants to have children, it is essential that she move to a bigger house with a back yard.

"I said I don't think it is." she counters. "Because in fact that just encourages you to stay at home and not go outside with your kid. If I live here with a child, I will be taking it across to Carlton Gardens all the time to the playground there because I'll need some space and they'll need to run around. And then maybe I'll meet other mothers and hang out and make new connections and build a bit of community."

Mitra is an urban planner but she also happens to have grown up at Bodhi Farm, the intentional community I visited in New South Wales. In fact, it was a wonderfully serendipitous moment when we realised that Mitra's Dad is Stu - the person who first told me about dadirri. I ask her whether she thinks Cairo can be considered a community.

"When you decide to become a member of Bodhi Farm," she says, "you're signing up for something quite intentionally and that is to be involved in community. You commit yourself to that through your programme of activity, which is weekly workdays, weekly meals, monthly meetings, AGMs. You are intentionally signing up to a lifestyle and you can't get membership at Bodhi Farm without being conscious of that and wanting to do that and agreeing to do that. Otherwise the community wouldn't work."

I nod in agreement. That's just what many people in community have been telling me. Participation is key.

"If you want to buy or rent an apartment here, there is no questionnaire asking do you want to have a communal life. In fact, this building was designed to enable single men to come to the city to have a more private life than they would if they had to go to a boarding house. This was one of the first opportunities in that era for people on low incomes who were moving to the city to access jobs or education to not have to live in shared accommodation. It was purposefully private. So you have your little private kitchenette and in fact, even though there was a communal dining hall, you could just order your meal from the communal dining hall and have it delivered to the box. You didn't have to open the door to access your food. None of the flats face onto each other so its really quite conscious of creating privacy and dignity in that privacy. I think it's really necessary in a big city to be able to retreat, so you can take a breath without feeling like you have to engage in conversation, and in doing that maybe you have more energy when you go outside to be communal. So you go join a beekeeping club or a music class or a drama group. We go to the park over the road with our friends to have picnics all the time. It's really convenient but when we come back home it's private space."

I'm still nodding, I'm excited because I know that the tension between public and private space is a huge cause of conflict in intentional communities. Maybe it always has been between neighbours. Mitra is offering me a different perspective. One that is driven by the viewpoint of a trained urban planner. I want to hear more, so I hold my tongue between my teeth to stop myself interrupting and let Mitra speak.

"It's all about ensuring that outside of the private developments you have opportunities that encourage you to be communal. We have the benefit here at Cairo of not only living in a building that was designed with that philosophy, we live in a part of the city that was also designed to give generous open public spaces. We have Carlton Gardens across the road which has really nice spaces to sit on the grass underneath the trees; there's a playground; there's a museum... the whole park is designed for people to go and spend time in and to enjoy. What we don't have so much of in Melbourne (and I think we could do much better) is the public square, the public open semi-commercial space. There are some really fundamental design principles that make these spaces good for hanging out in. How big they are, how much sun they get, the aspect, what is

NEIGHBOURS

designed at the ground floor in terms of uses, cafés and retail shops, maybe libraries, a mix of public and private spaces. Maybe fountains - something soothing and calming to offset the noise and chatter. Obviously, the best examples of those are in Europe and across the Middle East where, again, their dwellings aren't very big. A lot of life is lived outside and there is an opportunity to wander outside your flat and hang out in the public realm. And that is a passive encouragement of community and connection and belonging."

In my mind I've travelled to Barcelona, where we spent those few days when Husband was invited for an interview. It was early January, but the squares were still full of people hanging out in the sun. There were so many cafés, all with outside terraces. There were kids running around and old folk taking sun on a bench or playing boules. There were even outside table-tennis tables. When I think back to life in Britain, outside spaces have become meaner in recent years. Less grass and more concrete. Mitra confirms my thoughts.

"There's been a trend to design public open spaces to NOT loiter in. To NOT lie in. To NOT sit in. They put these little balls on the seats so you can't lie down on them. Or they make them sloping so you don't want to sit on them for very long. They make parks really open with lots of lights so there's nowhere really to linger or to feel like you're secluded at all, or you have any sense of wanting to stop and wait. That's supposed to be a crime-prevention activity but in fact it's also an anti-community activity. They are no longer places where you want to spend a nice time in. As opposed to purposefully creating a space where you actually want to spend some time, like putting some bocce courts, or some benches, or a reclining chair. There's a really good example of this in Collingwood, where there's a little pocket park and there are some benches for reclining that just scream "Come and lie down on me and spend time in the sun and be a bit frivolous!".

Now that she's saying it, it seems so important. How much of our shared public space has been commercialised or taken into private owner-

HIRAETH

ship? Shopping malls might be the modern equivalent of the traditional piazza, but whose space is it really? Isn't this a new form of enclosure? [19] 'Enclosing' common space for private profit? What happens to our relationship to land and to each other when we are forced to spend all our time in private spaces? Loneliness seems an inevitable outcome and the cynic in me whispers that this is the intention. When people are isolated, they have to spend money to socialise. What's more, they turn to consuming for comfort. Food, alcohol, drugs. Starved of human and cultural connection, we look to feed our soul elsewhere. It's not an accident that strong drinks are often referred to as 'spirits'.

Up in the forest behind the meditation hut, tall trees filter harsh sunlight and the fresh fragrance of eucalyptus enlivens the air. On the forest floor, tiny flowers bloom as though in an alpine meadow. Long green stems supporting a hand of yellow petals or white stars. Plump purple posies. I clamber onto a great round rock. Gray and sage green lichen stains its skin. My eyes follow an ant as long as my thumb as he makes his busy way. This morning in meditation, I felt an easeful focus. Mind drawing in. Body comfortable. Hearing, yet not reaching out to sounds. Thoughts arriving at the edge of my concentration and then pausing, as if in respect for what is happening. Alone in the beauty of the moment. I can see how I might make a life, here in Australia. I can see the years extending easily into the future. But a change is looming. After a third attempt, Husband has been shortlisted for a position in Barcelona. It is time to make a decision whether to stay or leave, and we know which it will be. We have another year here at most. As this thought arises, I'm amazed to feel sadness. Only a short time ago I was longing for home. For Wales. As I sit in the growing heat of this Australian noon, I conclude that there is only one place to live, and that is in the present.

In the afternoon session, I venture some feedback on yesterday's 'inquiry'. I tell how, when shame was mentioned, I heard my mother's voice telling me 'You ought to be ashamed of yourself!" The teacher, once again,

NEIGHBOURS

is Carol.

"How does it feel to hear your mother's voice like that?" I shrink down in my seat, an actions that indicates how small I feel.

"Then what happens?" Carol asks. I cup my hands over my eyes and open my fingers a little so I can see out. "Then I peep out at people" I say. "You peep out" she repeats "And how is it when you are stared at yourself?"

I look around at this room full of my colleagues, my community, my sangha. Some people looking back at me, at us, perched at the front on our cushions. Some with their eyes closed in concentration. "It's ok, sometimes."

"And other times?"

"Other times I need to be prepared"

"How do you prepare yourself?" Carol asks.

I mime a breast plate closing over my front. "I put on my armour."

Carol holds my gaze. Keeps holding it. I gaze back, unflinching. It is warm in her eyes. She regards me without judgment. Without holding back. We stay there for a long moment, just looking at each other, into each others' eyes.

After what feels like a few minutes, I smile. The intense energy of our gaze relaxes. "What have you learned?" she asks.

"I don't need my armour".

"You don't need your armour". She nods slowly, still seeing me.

During the silent walking meditation that follows, a door slams behind me and I find myself wondering "Who can that be?" My judging mind leaps into action and I feel tension lift my shoulders. A flash of insight shows me a clear pattern of behaviour. "That's how I build my armour! I criticise other people, and use the feeling of self-righteousness to build a defence!"

I see immediately how this habit creates distance. How it fosters pride and fear and a sense of separation. It feels like a light has gone on. Maybe all the walls we build, all the hedges and boundaries and borders we defend, are built to hide our own sense of shame. So that our neighbours don't see us for who we really are.

During the evening meditation, the room stills and quietens into a rarefied state of peace. I can hear the gentle night sounds of nature leaking through the walls. I settle onto my cushion, body relaxed and comfortable, dropping quickly into a state of deep concentration. It is sometimes this way after the first few days of retreat, when the busyness of everyday mind has fallen away and the noble silence of practice has taken up residence in my heart. As an added inquiry to the instructions offered by the teacher, I feel curious about what and who I might be beneath my armour. Would it be possible to remove it all? Every scrap of it? And if so, what will I find beneath? I begin to mentally pick at my protective psychic shield, imagining it as a skin-tight covering. I pull back a corner and peel it away. Pick at the edges and pull it off in strips. It's a bit like preparing for decorating - taking away all the old wallpaper, scraping at discoloured paint. I spend a full thirty minutes at this work, intensely focused but somehow still conscious of the warm, supportive presence of my fellow meditators. Somewhere towards the end of the session, a chink of light appears underneath a section of armour. I keep tugging and what is revealed is pure brightness. Under all that protective padding, inside the barrier that I have painstakingly built up over years and now equally painstakingly unravelled, is a luminosity that seems to sing with infinite depth. There is no limit to this radiance. It is bound only by the appearance of me, which feels increasingly fragile and threadbare. I sit for the rest of the session, entranced by this edgeless, boundless version of myself, sensing my human skin as mere container. Basking in this understanding feels utterly safe. Utterly soothing. I could stay here for ever, with no need for the strange, awkward appendage of mortal body. I come to realise that my face is smiling, a laugh is playing in my belly and no wonder. Life is showing itself to be a gigantic joke and this small self I drag about the world is no more than an unwitting ingenue. When the bell for the end of the session rings and my companions file silently out into the darkness, I ease myself back on my cushions and lie rapt, engrossed in the absurd brilliance of it all.

NEIGHBOURS

Traditional dance - Phillip Island

Chapter *11*

Deep Listening

"It means listening not just with your ears, but with your eyes and your heart."

Making our way across empty beach, sun giving its last light, we climb, a group of twenty or so excited nature-lovers, onto a rugged clifftop. All around us, a babbling is beginning in the grasslands. The birds are coming in to nest.

"Sit down", says Graham, the ranger. "You'll see why in a minute."

We crouch on the sandy path and moments later, a shower of busy wings emerges from the darkening sky. A flurry of shearwater birds flap and flutter overhead, diving in from their long day at sea to find rest in their familiar burrows. Only nature is guiding these birds. Some inner radar telling them exactly where to go - where on this whole blue-black cliff top their hungry young are waiting. Crouched in the cool, sandy earth we sit in awe, welcoming each bird as it scooters in to land. I pull my hood tight around my face, fearful of claws or wings catching in my hair. It is too dark now for my camera to focus and I surrender to the moment, allowing the strange beauty to utterly prevail. The whole show lasts about fifteen minutes.

Back in the education room, we watch as the ranger points out the flight path of the birds. He has managed to track a single male all the way to Greenland and back. Arriving back on Australian shores, the male will find a mate and father a single egg. The devoted parents will take it in turns to fly south to Antarctica to fill their bird bellies with protein-rich krill. The male will take first turn on the nest, allowing mum to re-fuel after her delivery. Then they will swap, each spending days in the krill fields, putting on weight and bringing home food for their chick. When March comes around, the parents will take a last visit to Antarctica to fuel up before embarking on their 12,000km trip north. Graham the ranger points out their route. First a stop-over in Japan, then all the way up to the Bering Strait, where they will make their summer home. The November return of the shearwater is predictable almost to a day and the locals have devised a gathering to welcome them. It's a community festival of song, spoken word and performance. Local Aboriginal elders are in demand but Aunty Doris Paton, whose ancestors belonged to these parts, is kind enough to grant me an interview. She tells how her people used to camp here for months, feasting on 'mutton birds', as the shearwater are known. Then, like the birds, the tribe moved on to another landscape, to another source of food.

"To know when the birds are back, when the eggs are there, this listening and knowing is the essence of dadirri", she says. "It means listening not just with your ears, but with your eyes and your heart."

Both the birds and the Aboriginal people have this instinctive and intimate relationship with their environment. They move as and when they need to, guided by the turning of the seasons and some silent inner wisdom.

Aunty Doris tells me that the word dadirri is not from her language. To get to the source, I need to seek out Miriam-Rose, the elder whose video I watched on the internet, speaking about dadirri in a way that made the hairs on my forearm crackle. I make a phone call to the Catholic education site on which her video is embedded and they say they will try to get a message to her. I know enough about Aboriginal culture by now to know that this might take some time! After a month or so, I phone the Catholic institution again.

"Why don't you call the school?" they suggest, helpfully. "I can do that?" I squeak. "I can just call her?"

Speaking to Miriam on the phone is like conversing with spirit. Somehow, I hardly believed that this woman exists, let alone imagined that I might speak with her. I force myself to listen closely to the undulations of her voice as she tells me about her experience with dadirri. By the time I ring off, my face is wet with tears. I want to meet with her. By chance, there is an opportunity coming up to do just that by way of a week-long visit to where Miriam lives in the Northern territory town of Nauiyu.

Nauiyu is a community of neat, square-ish houses spread out over about thirty acres of land. Between the houses, a sealed road winds, taking the eye into a surrounding landscape of rolling parkland. A small boy cycles up and over the bumpy terrain, becoming little more than a speck as he pedals as far as he can go. On a full scale football pitch, a dozen lithe, barefoot youngsters kick a ball about.

On the first morning together as group, we gather at the riverbank. Miriam has arranged for two women from the community to perform a welcome ceremony. It's for us, but it's also for the ancestors, to let them know that we are here. We are instructed to stand with our feet in the shallows, which is an act of faith, considering they have just been pointing out the eerie slide marks of a crocodile's tail. Fearless, Agnes and Bridget stand out further into the flow of the river and call to the river spirits, their language sounding like the gentle burbling of the water itself. When they turn back to face us, they anoint each of us in turn with water from their river - first our foreheads, then our bellies, having us lift our shirts to receive the blessing at the place we connected to our mother.

Reflecting afterwards on the experience from the safety of the riverbank, we are accompanied by the slow wheeling overhead of large brown hawks, which Agnes insists is an auspicious sign. The river rushes on, as Miriam tries to explain its significance in the community.

"So much of our culture depends on the river. Not only water for drinking, but food, too. Like fish and crocodile eggs."

When she shows us her paintings later, we can see this importance for ourselves. Along with native animals, plants and significant features of the local landscape, the river is central. Patterns of life, stories and legends are all told through these paintings and everyone, it seems, is an artist. In the warmth of the afternoon, women gather with canvas, paint and brushes and an exhibition at the school shows how young talent is fostered. Each painting has an artist bio and a price-tag. In spite of complicated social issues, Aboriginal art, at least, is taken seriously. What's more, it fetches good money. For many, it is a way out of material poverty. Dance is also highly valued and we are invited to an unique performance by the children of the village.

Lean brown bodies smeared with white ochre, heads and loins encircled with bold red cloth, they appear somewhat shyly. To one side, a small group of adult musicians start a slow, rhythmic beat before the didge player, painted in the same white ochre as the young dancers, begins playing his low, resonant tone. Maintaining the rhythm on traditional clap sticks, the men start to gather up a pace and the crowd - visitors at one end and locals at the other, applaud and cheer as the boys stamp and gesture their way across the grassy stage. Their confidence grows as the didge starts to bounce a tune, their movements become more and more animated, faces beaming with energy and delight. One handsome youngster risks a perfectly-timed, cheeky flick of the head, invoking hoots of laughter. This is a performance, but Miriam is solemn when she informs us that these boys are reviving ancient traditions. For fifteen years, there has been no dancing in this community.

Towards the end of the show, we are invited - first men and then women - to dance alongside them. The men make wide spear-throwing movements, stamp their feet into the red earth and hoot loudly, while the women's dance is altogether more demure. To invite us in this way is truly a gesture of friendship. Of reconciliation. The deep symbolism of this hospitality is not lost on us.

In the evening, we are treated to damper - scone-like breads cooked on an open fire. We sit in a circle, slapping at mosquitos, and then the stories begin, yarning up, as they say, long into the night. Everyone here knows how to tell a story and as far as antagonists go, you can't get much better than a crocodile. In one tale, a woman fishing by the river hits the croc with a turtle, but loses her ring finger to the animal.
In another, a man gets taken by a crocodile whilst fishing in the river and they tussle, Dundee-style, until the fisherman, having followed his elders' advice to keep his fingernails long, manages to escape by gouging out the eyes of the croc.
The tale must have been told a hundred times before but like eager children hearing their favourite book at bedtime, the audience cheer and clap their appreciation. An oral culture for perhaps fifty thousand years, this is how the Aboriginals and we, once upon a time, passed on culture and wisdom.

The following day finds us sitting again with Miriam by the river, much as disciples might have sat with the Buddha. She talks about the meaning of dadirri and the way we can practice it in our lives, describing dadirri as a deep inner spring. She points to the river and says how the river is fed by many small springs.

"If the springs dry up", she says, "the river will die. It's the same for us. If we don't have time for ourselves, to listen to and be with this spring we have inside us, we will die."
In the language of Miriam's family, her tribal name means "deep water calling to deep". She shakes her head, still amazed at this sign that this teaching is what she was born to offer.

Australia is slow to recognise it, but the perpetuity of Aboriginal spiritual life needs to be at the heart of any way forward. In separating Aboriginal people from their lands, whitefellas took away their relationship to Country. The disorientation and sense of disconnection brought about by life away from the people, animals and landscape of their community remains as a feeling of groundlessness, even though now, many Aboriginal people have lived several generations in cities.

This disorientation is not unique to Aboriginal people. In some way, everyone living without a close connection to the earth, to where their food comes from and to other people is in some way experiencing a sense of false separation. False because the truth is that we rely on the earth, we are part of it and if we don't experience it regularly, then we can forget. Devoid of these relationships, we experience a sense of hiraeth. Of deep longing. It might show up as sadness or pain, anxiety or depression. In a poignant and timely reminder of what indigenous spirituality has to offer, Miriam-Rose emphasises self-reflection, respect for country and for each other. As Miriam explicitly states, it's not only Aboriginals who benefit from a re-learning of this knowledge. It is the Aboriginal people's gift to all of Australia, perhaps even to the world.

Of course, dadirri is not the only way to understand this. As with all mystical teachings, the wisdom of dadirri is not only offered in one culture. In the Welsh bardic or poetic mythology of my own ancestors, the word *awen* is translated as 'muse'. A sister word, *annwn* can mean 'the otherworld' or simply 'very deep place.' Druidic bards or poets could enter the place of annwn and receive the blessing of awen, inspiration. In our materialistic world, we ignore these deep places at our peril. Grounded in logic and science, our modern world works principally with that which can be seen, touched and proven. Less valued are these realms of the imaginal, the spirit, the unseen. Less valued, art and poetry. In our quest for control, have we closed the doors on soulfulness? Have we shut ourselves off from these deep wells of belonging?

As the Ghan train carries me slowly south towards Alice Springs, what I am carrying away is the strong, steady presence of Miriam. I carry the quiet togetherness of the women as they sit together on the ground, painting. In my ears is the wheel and cry of the hawks overhead and behind my eyes, the rolling green grassland and leafy spaciousness of the Nauiyu community. Images of young children with liquid brown eyes and spontaneous smiles. Supple brown feet, moving with a sure connection to the earth they know so intimately. Silent nods of hello. An upturned palm as query. The raise of an eyebrow. The click of a tongue. Elegant eloquence. Gentle being-ness. I store it deep inside myself and hope that I can call on it when later, back in the busy city, I am in need of grace.

At Alice Springs Backpackers Lodge, the air is crisp and cold. An air conditioning unit sits on the wall, a reminder of my time in the humid north. My time in Nauiyu - the heat, the mosquitos, is all beginning to feel like a dream.

Uluru, Australia

Chapter *12*

At the Centre of it All

"Under the watchful gaze of the Rock, everything is made holy."

A man stands bare-foot at the base of the Rock, holding a bell. When he strikes it, the sound resonates up and away, taking our gaze along the huge ochre-coloured monolith and up into the constant blueness of sky. He walks carefully, meditatively, immersed in a prayerful weaving of respect. We turn our backs on the tourist hubbub and follow him. Surely, this is what the Rock demands of us? Like the Anangu people, traditional custodians of Uluru, we instinctively understand that this natural phenomenon, standing silent and majestic in the centre of the desert, is a place for sacred ceremony.

That afternoon, when his Holiness the Dalai Lama arrives in Mutjitjulu, the village closest to the monolith, a crowd is waiting for him at the school ground. Sitting on the warm earth under a baking sun, a couple of hundred people have just finished chanting the mantra known throughout his homeland of Nepal and Tibet.
"Om mani padme hum."
The red earth sings along with us.

The Dalai Lama is nothing more or less than himself. Amused and

HIRAETH

amusing, he watches the ceremonial dances with delighted curiosity, before reaching out to touch the face of one of the Aboriginal performers. "We have different noses" he giggles. "but underneath, we are the same." He goes on to remark how Aboriginal people are connected to the earth in a way that many humans have forgotten. He speaks simply of the need for us to rediscover this connection so that we will be moved to take care of the planet.

After his talk, we join a throng of attendees on a hill overlooking this small town. In the distance, Uluru glows redder as the sun dips in the darkening sky. Some take the opportunity to chant Buddhist prayers. Others toast the moment with champagne. Under the watchful gaze of the Rock, everything is made holy.

Husband and I want to immerse ourselves in the landscape of Central Australia, so we take off on a hike which carries us from Alice Springs into the West McDonnell ranges, along the Larapinta Trail. Our packs are challengingly heavy, as we have to carry not only our camping gear and food for the four day trip, but also quite a few litres of water. My pack may be heavy, but my being feels light as we step into the gold and umber heart of this vast continent.

The afternoon takes us through rocky red vallies flanked by long, low-slung mountains. In the creation story told by the local Arrentes tribe, this mountain range is a caterpillar, crawling across the desert landscape. The sky overhead spreads a delicate rose tint, then breaks into sunburnt orange and suddenly, it is dark, the canopy overhead speckled with stars. "Guess what time it is?" asks Husband. "7.30!" There's little else to do but to climb into our sleeping bags. We leave the fly sheet off, so we can contemplate the night sky. A shooting star, then another, falls magically across the scene and before we know it, we're both sound asleep. At 3am, I wake again, shivering. The moon has risen silently behind us and is throwing her blue-white gaze over the desert. In this light, the pale bark of ghost gums stands out bright against the blue-black void of sky. I can see perfectly as I unzip the tent and climb out to pee. The air puckers my skin in an icy chill. Wisps of clouds have appeared at the edges of the mountain top, and it feels eerie and special and I want to take a photo, but it's far too cold to faff about with exposures so I hurry back to huddle into the tent. Husband is awake now too and we lie giggling with excitement, unnerved by a sense of deep water running beneath the dry river on which we have made our bed. We are completely alone in the middle of the Australian desert.

Towards afternoon on the second day, glints of quartz in sandy soil become shining rocks, as though the whole ground holds a precious secret. As well as meeting very few people or animals, vegetation is sparse. At one dry river bed, I spot a tiny purple flower bravely poking her head out from the sand - sure proof of the underground water we sensed last night. The bright violet petals contrast sharply with a palette of grey-white, green and red but as we walk on, the terrain changes colour again. Rocks underfoot become a verdant garden, young gums mingling with yellow brush. Our bodies feel both looser and stronger, although blisters are appearing on both heels and toes. The weight of my pack has become part of my body. My feet have fallen into a rhythm. My mind, too, is settling into ease.

During the first day, I was busy editing the images I had gathered up north. I spent the day thinking about what went well, what I missed, what I would do differently. But during this second day, my mind has quietened, allowing the sound and silence of the desert to penetrate my being. I hear bird song and the gentle whisper of breeze through dry shrub. It's a lot like being on retreat. We make a brief lunch stop, but I find I like hiking with the warm sun overhead. Like a lizard, I'm soaking up heat to last me through the cold night to come. We follow the river bed through a narrow gorge. Dark red rocks tower up either side of us as we pick our way amongst tall trees and stony outcrops. After a couple of hours with only a narrow sky overhead, the gorge opens out in to a magnificent clearing. I

HIRAETH

spot an abandoned fire pit and as I turn to comment how this would make a great camp site, I see Husband has arrived at the same conclusion. I drop my pack. We have about an hour before dark and we set about cooking dinner. Soon, we are sitting before a glowing fire, eating curry and rice and watching the stars emerge. A deep silence falls and we sit, each in our own thoughts, until from far up on the hillside, we hear a sound which chills us more than the encroaching night air.

"Aoooouuuuuuuuuu!" Long and yearning, the howl of a dingo rebounds around the canyon walls. I nestle closer, feeling the fingers of fear tickle my neck and arms. When I turn to look at his face, my eyes wide, I can see that Husband, too, is unsettled. From behind us, closer and deep in the narrow gorge from which we came, another howl goes up. "Aouuuuuuuuuuooo!" We are surrounded.

Whilst reassuring me confidently that dingos are afraid of humans and don't tend to attack, Husband is reaching for his knife.

"They just want our food", he says, tucking the supply bag firmly into the tent. I feel safer by the fire, but sleeping there would mean sleeping in the open, so reluctantly we throw sand to douse the flames and crawl into the tent. Lying there in the dark, I remember Stu telling me how the Aboriginal men he works with are still afraid of the dark and often sleep with the light on.

"Their parents used to scare them with stories of spirits, to stop them wandering off from the camp." he explained.

Exposed as I feel now, I can understand the need to prevent small children from wandering around at night. How fearful their parents must have been! Wide awake inside the ancient mythology of this place, we decide it's a great opportunity to 'journey', and we settle down, preparing ourselves for a ritual meditation we were taught by a shaman in Wales.

Travelling in my mind, I go to the water source I always use to enter the dreamtime - the fresh water spring at Holts Field. No sooner have I stepped into the stream, I am carried way underground, under the earth and through its core, speeding through the centre of the planet to where

AT THE CENTRE OF IT ALL

I lie here on the desert floor. Dingos stalk the hills and I have a sense of my minuteness in the centre of this huge red desert, in the middle of this huge red continent, on this beautiful blue planet, in this great wide universe.

I've been away from Melbourne five weeks, from Wales more than two years. I am tired from hiking and from travelling. Lying in the dark, I realise how, in one way or another, all my various "homes" have dissolved. The home my parents first made for me. The home in which I spent my teenage years. The home I shared with my young family. The home I made for us in Holts Field. I think about how the Aboriginals eschewed a permanent place, preferring to live off the land and their wits. I think of the Dalai Lama and how he has lived exiled from his homeland and of the Buddha, abandoning the life of a householder to pursue the ultimate, eternal freedom. Even Henry David Thoreau, that modern-day, secular advocate of simple living, revered the life of the 'saunterer' - one who could wander without attachment to people or place. Perhaps for now, instead of being an unfortunate who has lost her homes, I am fortunate, lucky enough not to be bound by land or house. Perhaps my task right now is to realise the wealth of having a home I can carry with me everywhere. The home that Jess, my meditation teacher, was forever trying to bring us back to. That home inside.

Streetlamp, Spain

Chapter *13*

Becalmed

"Drinking in the solitude, in peaceful communion with land, I feel reassured that I am not completely mad."

Here I am again, launching a new film just before I leave the country. I have a little more time - months rather than days. Time enough to do a few more screenings after the launch. Our crowd fund has been successful in raising enough to cover publishing costs and I'm working with a designer friend on the cover.

During the making of Deep Listening, I have completely convinced myself of the power of listening. Our ancestors relied on this kind of listening not only for their health and well-being, but for their very survival. Listening to land, they gained knowledge of what the earth required in exchange for their food and clothing. Listening to others, they understood the needs of each person in their community. Listening to themselves, they saw their place within the whole. Listening like this, we, too, can bring ourselves into alignment with life.

My journey to make the Deep Listening documentary began with a question about how we might solve conflict and ends up being a teaching in how to build community through connection. I could say that this book began where the film ended, or that the book is an attempt to put what I learned making the film into practice. A living experiment, if you like. But when I finish the film, I don't know yet that there will be a book.

At the launch screening, I stand on stage to welcome a room packed full of people - many of whom I recognise. This is my Australian community. These are the people whose story the film is telling. Deep Listening (60min) is a documentary about alternative lifestyle in Australia, beginning with the famous Aquarius Festival and one of the first times that Aboriginals were asked for permission to use their land. It dances through different intentional communities - some rural, some urban - each with its own way of linking to the land, to each other and to local indigenous people. In the end, it was not so hard to weave an Aboriginal thread into the story. Turns out they were there all along. [20]

These last weeks fly by. Summer warms the streets and parks and the scent of jasmine infuses the air, making Melbourne feel tropical. Although evenings are still cool, the days are heating up and we spend Sunday afternoons lazing on a blanket in Carlton Gardens. We guzzle experiences, making the most of everything. "The last this, the last that..."

On the weekend before we leave, we go for dinner in a restaurant that has been a favourite during our time here. The ownership changed hands some time ago and on the menu, instead of our favourite Ukrainian dumplings, there is steak. We are relieved to find our usual corner nook still intact, so we tuck ourselves inside. The wallpaper still carries the names of restaurants from a Russian telephone book and our glasses still say "The Crimean" but we know this is the last time we will come here. As we toast the memories of ice-cold vodka from the freezer and delicate engraved glasses sticky with walnut liqueur, I am surprised to see that Husband's eyes, like mine, are moist.
"Things are changing even before we go." he mourns.

BECALMED

Hot wind wafting in from the desert caresses my bare legs as I cycle through North Fitzroy. At CERES, I help pull out the zabutons and lay them in a circle, placing a cushion on each one. I take my place next to Jess, feeling the gravitas of this final sit. The room has filled up. Forty-odd people facing each other in a wide circle. Doors and windows are flung open and ceiling fans swipe the air gently, causing a cool breeze to float between us. My body feels grounded and heavy, but my heart is light. Entirely present, I feel no distress, no pain, no discomfort. I am held in this circle as if in a loving family. When it is time to walk, I head outside with the others, bare feet kissing the earth. Leaf litter from gum trees sticks to my soles and I look up to see tall branches waving in the graduated evening sky. With a broad, relaxed gaze, I take in my colleagues moving slowly, like sleepwalkers, their attention focused.

"Last time at CERES", I think. Tears prickle, and I allow them to fall freely down my cheeks.

Inside, Jess speaks passionately about sangha, of how we are all held in a worldwide circle. She reminds us how we can turn inside for refuge, to that safe place. How we can be held by it, comforted by it, fed and nourished by it. I recall how, in a recent workshop, Jess spoke of the need for us, as teachers and facilitators, to 'step up' and I wonder, in this new phase of life, what that might come to mean for me. Approaching my fiftieth year on this planet, is it time to 'step up' to being an elder? And what, in this world, does that even mean?

***

"*De donde eres?*" It's a question I get asked a lot.

"*Soy de Gales*" I say. "I'm from Wales."

But when I think of home, I am as likely, at this time, to think of our little flat in Melbourne. It's confusing.

"*Y donde vives?*" I explain that I live in *Barrio Gótico*, but I know that it is not home. If you have been to Barcelona, you will have visited the Gothic quarter. It is part of the old town, near the port. The narrow streets have their charm, but in the daytime, the tall buildings block out light and in our apartment, it is dark and chilly. Day and night, throngs of tourists pass underneath our first floor window, trundling truculent wheelie cases across ancient cobbled stones. At the other end of our street is an ancient, ornate cathedral that seems to be impossible to pass without taking a souvenir selfie. It causes a near-permanent bottleneck. I stay home a lot, staring at the Roman walls of my bedroom or lost in high-speed internet. There are fibre optic cables under those cobblestones.

On Barceloneta beach, a group of old folk gather to play dominos and enjoy the winter sun. Some of them swim every day, plunging their all-over tans into clear water and emerging dripping, breath heavy, muscles twitching from cold. Watching them brings to mind the group of swimmers in Wales and I join them once or twice, practising my few phrases of *castellano* and enjoying a brief sense of community. Renewed by a dip in the sea, I feel momentarily at peace with this new life, but even with the beach nearby, I'm finding it difficult. Between cloudless sky and boundless sea, there is plenty of blue, but not hardly enough green.

We spend Christmas Day on this beach, with Husband's impressive new workplace looming behind us. He is stoked, posting morning photos from his seafront office window and the sunset on his way home. One day, he shares a snap of the intricately decorated, domed ceiling of the post office on the corner of our street and although I frequent that building often, I realise with a jolt that I have never noticed the elaborate architecture. Wrapped in my bell jar bubble, I have stopped engaging with my surroundings.

On the weekends, I spend a thankful few hours at Can Masdeu, an old leper hospital that has been home to a community of anarchists since 2001. This huge, white building sits high above the city, surrounded by forest and gardens.

Working alongside others as part of a permaculture project, I put my

BECALMED

hands in the dry, crumbly soil to help grow food in what they call a *jardín comestible*. This is therapy. Literally grounding. It's perhaps the one place, other than actually in the sea, where I feel happy. When the work is done, we share a lazy lunch around a long table in the courtyard. A lively, multi-lingual conversation touches on subjects dear to me. Community. Sustainability. Not just interesting concepts, these are a way of life. In this place, I feel understood, valued, and it is in this place that one day, whilst crouching to weed a vegetable bed, my friend tells me gently that I seem to have "lost my spirit".

Needing to escape the city, I book a solitary retreat at Ecodharma, an eco-spiritual community high up in the Catalan Pyrenees. Drinking in the quiet, alone in peaceful communion with land, I feel reassured that I am not, after all, going mad. What I am suffering from is treatable, even curable. What I need is to get back into nature.

When my cousin comes to visit, he takes out a sailing boat, crossing the hazy horizon back and forth across the bay before the vessel seems to stall. We who are left on the shore wonder if something has gone wrong but when he returns, sunburned and smiling, he explains this stilling as the sailor's state of being 'becalmed'. It is a state when a ship has no wind in its sails and loses all momentum. Now that the activity of travelling is over, I recognise in myself this stalled state of being. I am yearning for a new project, a new focus, but the process refuses to be rushed.
"How does a sailor deal with this state of no wind?' I ask my cousin. "She waits.' he replies, matter-of-factly. "The wind will come again."

Shadows in Winter

Chapter *14*

The Husband's Tale

"It must be hard having someone watch you be sad all the time."

"Look" she says, pointing to the winter sunlight on the black iron handle on the bathroom door. I follow her gaze and then follow it back, back to her face, creased from an awkward night's sleep. She was awake again, not just because the bed collapsed - again - but because the fear got her. Again. Where does this fear come from? I have never known this woman to be fearful. Where is Wife? Like the shaft of light on the freshly-painted door, I see glimpses of her, which, foolishly, I trust and fall headlong into, before they are snatched away by some personality I do not know. Yes, it is human, and female, this being with whom I share my life, but it is not the woman I married.

In any situation of conflict, the first necessity is to apportion blame.
We used to joke about this. It was something Carol Perry said in one of her workshops. I don't get everything Wife comes out with - it's a little way out for me - but as a way of getting underneath the seriousness of an argument, this works. Now, as the blame mounts up, the joke is wearing thin.

HIRAETH

It's my fault for taking her away from her community, from her son, from her cat, from her job, from her life. She doesn't say this, but instead blames herself for leaving - a blame which makes its way back around to me, since I was the one with the far away job offer.

"You are an adult." I say. "You made your own decisions."

This is me, trying to relieve myself of the blame she is not expressly directing at me. Why can't either of us just say what we mean?

On a day not unlike today, winter light thrown across the room, we are huddled under a blanket, both sick with some kind of bug. Illness has brought low our defences and while we are chatting, half-enjoying the enforced closeness, she says it. She's not angry. It's more like a musing but it gives voice to the thing we've both been silently thinking.

"I wonder if marrying you was a mistake?"

As soon as she has said it, we are kissing. Despite the snot and sweaty moistness we are embracing. A physical apology for even thinking that thought. And yet there it is. She has said it and yes, I admit, I have thought it.

Sometime later, one of us, I forget which, points out the date, and we see that it's the anniversary of our wedding. Two years ago, we were hiking on Wilsons Prom. Two years before that, we were dancing in Buenos Aires. Two years before that, we were making promises before a small group of friends in a registry office in Cardiff, before wandering through a sunny park to a reception laced with vodka and tango. What had I done to that carefree woman? That grounded, powerful, capable, brilliant (that's our little joke) woman I get to call Wife? I miss her. And I'm terrified that it's my fault she's gone.

Those little noticings. The pointing to the winter light and the wondering about whether we should have married, this is her trying to work it out. She is as confused as I am as to what has happened. The other day, she sent me an article about menopause and to be honest, it was spot

THE HUSBAND'S TALE

on. Not only the hot flushes and night sweats, everyone knows about those, but the myriad of other symptoms. Crushing anxiety, panic attacks, desolate depression, weariness, overwhelm, an inability to cope with even the smallest of tasks. If it's frustrating for me, what must it be like for her? If I am losing my wife, then she is losing her self. I can only imagine what that feels like.

And yet, the truth is that whatever the causes, her condition leaves me holding it all. Full-time job, plus all the bills and foreign paperwork. I thought she'd be quicker to pick up the language. To find her feet here. Also, I was pretty sure that we both agreed to buy this little *casita*. Did I imagine that too? The location is perfect - I can get to work in the city without too much hassle and she has the solace of both forest and beach. Most importantly, we can afford it. There's a lot of work to do but we're up for that. Or at least, we were. The reality of sleeping in a cold house without hot running water in winter is admittedly a challenge, even for me. In Melbourne, I used to sing her a little song when I went off to work in the morning.
"Bye bye wife. Bye bye happiness. Hello loneliness, I think I'm going to cry. Bye bye my wife goodbye."
I meant it. Though I enjoy my job, we had such fun together. Now, every morning I'm relieved to leave the house and I get the feeling she's glad to see me go. It must be hard having someone watch you be sad all the time. At least when I am gone she can arrange her face how she wants it, without any pressure to make it smile.

Villa Mimosa, Catalunya

Chapter 15

Villa Mimosa

"If there is any joy in all this, it happens in the small moments."

How does a person wait for the wind to come and fill her sails? How does a sailor navigate the inner and outer frustrations of being 'in the doldrums?'. How do we learn to be with uncertainty? How, now, does the writer sit with the blank page?

In any Heroine's Journey, there is a place, right before Sovereignty and The Way Forward, where one last adventure turns out to be almost fatal. In the Flores model, this is where All is Lost, and in her book *Women who Run with the Wolves*, psychologist and *cantadora* Clarissa Pinkola Estes names it as a time when a wolf-woman has 'lost the scent' and is looking around here, there and everywhere for her pack. This is me then, in Spain, looking here, there and everywhere for where, and to whom, I belong. It's a painful, drawn out search which involves, in mythological terms, a full descent.

For me, it happened to be the menopause, combined with moving to a different country, but it could have been one of any number of life events that sent me plummeting. Because what is clear to me now, is that mid-life, as much as birth, puberty, adulthood, marriage, and death, is a rite of passage. If we are lucky to still be alive, we will be asked to undergo an initiation, and initiations always take place in the dark. In the legends, seekers are led into underground places - caves, tunnels and the like. Or else they are blindfolded. What's more, there is always the instruction never to look back. Initiation demands that we stay a while in the unknown - neither seeing the way forward or behind. Unable to go either ahead nor back, we are meant to stay still. To go down.

Going down in this way requires courage and faith. Courage to face that which we fear most, and faith that we will emerge, or at least that it will be worth the trouble. But faith is something that our modern age does not preach. The gods offered to us in this era of late capitalism are the gods of money. We identify as consumers and upon consumption, we build our identity. Wealth is power. Property is power. Status is power. But these are masculine forms of power. They are shallow and untrustworthy sources of refuge, and they serve us poorly.

In the Sumerian myth *The Descent of Inanna*, the goddess Inanna enters into the Underworld after hearing her sister Ereshkigal's cries from the Great Below. Inanna travels through seven gates, at each threshold offering up one of her worldly powers. During her journey, she experiences a deep transformation, uniting with a sister-self who has been living in darkness. This can be seen as Inanna shedding her more patriarchal-defined identities and re-discovering her deep feminine self. Surrendering power-over in favour of power-from-within. When her shadow self Ereshkigal is finally heard and seen, both Inanna and her sister experience profound shifts in consciousness. [21]

During these times of our own global shift in consciousness, we are being asked to take a long, hard look at our behaviour. At the way we operate and the effect we have on the world. We are asked to realign with our ethical values, but what are those values? What is it that we hold dear? Who told us how we should and shouldn't behave? Upon whose authority do we act? Inanna is asked to surrender all the ways she uses her power to harm others and even the ways she harms herself when she fails to speak her truth. By the time she re-gains these powers, she has undergone purification and is more aligned to her true path. Which all sounds great, but we all know how hard it can be to let go of what we believe in, and what an emptiness can be left if we do choose to let it go. Is it the emptiness that most scares us?

In another mythical tale that Heather-Jo Flores likes to tell, King Arthur's Knight Sir Gawain (following some dramatic twists and turns) finds happiness when he extends his wife the freedom to make decisions over her own life. Offered this freedom, what is it we choose? Do we stay in relative safety of the old ways, even though they are no longer serving us? Or can we dive deep and emerge with some new wisdom?

In many spiritual traditions, it is said that what you are searching for, is also searching for you. When Villa Mimosa gazes up from a page in one of my super-fast internet searches, is that casita waiting for me? The house, a run-down holiday home on the edge of Garraf National Park, has been empty for ten years. It needs an owner prepared to take on the substantial work of renovation and although this is daunting, it's easy to see why this casita appeals. It's a lot like my chalet in Wales.

When we travel down from Barcelona for a viewing, we take some time to sit in the local *plaça*, watching children play in the car-free roads, enjoying a *cortado* and imagining what it would be like to live here. With the idea of trying it out before we commit, we agree to rent the house next door and before I know it, we have bought a car and moved all our stuff out of the city. The sale of the house progresses slowly, because it seems that as well as being on the edge of town, it is also on the edge of being legal. There are a few glitches to sort out before we sign the papers. In a further complication, we have lost a chunk of our UK savings in the economic fallout following the *Brexit* vote to take the UK out of the EU.

Despite all this, Husband is keen. Between emails and permits and lawyers, he seems confident it will all work out. But I have a vision of myself from that time, standing in the cool downstairs room of our rented house, drenched in sweat and shaking with fear.

We sign the documents at the beginning of September, celebrating with a glass of cava on a cafe terrace near the lawyer's office in Barcelona's Passeig de Gràcia. The clash between our dilapidated property and the elegant architecture around us is stark. I feel under-dressed and unfit for purpose. Are we going to be able to pull this off?

The weather is still hot and dry when we take everything out of the casita, filling the garden with remnants from someone else's life. I am wavering, focusing on small details to get me through each day. We have only a few ideas as to how this plan will progress, but one thing I can see clearly is that underneath the dark, dingy grime is an original wooden floor. With a rare burst of energy, I insist that we sand it down before we move in. We rent an industrial sander from a local equipment shop and work all night until it is done. In a strange twist of fate, my cousin is here to help, bringing a welcome breeze into my flagging sails. Varnishing this floor feels as though I am stroking the house to life. I am not okay with this yet, but I want to be. I want to skip the hard bit and have a comfortable home straight away, but as we begin the renovations, the house demands that we work at a more Spanish kind of pace. Clearly, it will be a while until we have even basic comforts. Committing to using as many natural and recycled materials as possible, each decision takes ages to research and consider. We need to wait for the right thing to come up, at a price we can afford. Winter comes and goes and still we don't have hot water or a proper bed.

In the system of design that is permaculture, it is said that living in a place for a full year allows for insight into the 'lay' of the land, the ways that nature merges with culture, such as the natural line of foot

VILLA MIMOSA

traffic through a property or the plants that thrive effortlessly. We don't need a whole winter to tell us we require hot water, but we do need a whole season to find a second-hand bath that will fit into the tiny bathroom space; to source a used cylinder that will accept a feed from both electric and solar powers; and to find a carpenter who 'gets' us. Until then, we wash with water heated in the kettle and on the wood burner, one person pouring while the other sits in the bath in a way that my grandmother would have recognised. Connecting to the internet is tricky up here in the woods and for a while, I seek out wifi in the local library and cafés. This has both up and down sides. On the one hand, I cannot disappear so easily into the distorted wonderland of internet searches and social media but, on the other, when I want to cry over Skype to my friend in Australia, I have to do it on the steps of the *biblioteca municipal.*

Once a week, we treat ourselves to a sauna and swim at the local sports centre. I come out feeling more human, softly glowing and relaxed. On these nights we make time to chat over Chinese food in the village and I seem to sleep more soundly, despite not having a proper bed. The fold-out sofa on which we are sleeping was not made for everyday use and after it finally collapses, we switch to an air bed on the floor. It serves just about well enough, and when I think I can't stand it any more, I remember the people I filmed living in caravans in damp Welsh fields while they built their innovative homes by hand. While I never questioned their dedication to the cause, I have now elevated them all to the status of heroes and heroines.

It is not lost on me that the name of our new house is Mimosa, which was also the name of the ship which, in the 1800's, took Welsh people across the world to create a new colony in Patagonia. Along the way, many people starved to death, unable to make that harsh, dusty land sustain them. They travelled all the way across the desert until they found the lush foothills of the Andes - a land which they better understood how to farm. Here, they thrived and their descendants are still living happily there today. Clarissa Estés talks about the 'gift of exile' - the way it strengthens

121 | 153

HIRAETH

us. But I am not feeling very strong.

If there is any joy in all this, it happens in the small moments, like when watching small birds coming to the feeder outside the window. Coal tits with shiny black waistcoats. Cheeky-looking crested tits with tufty mohicans. Larger brown jays, dapper with bright blue accessories. In these moments, I feel as though I could make a home here.
And then there's the sea. Always the sea. Calmer and less wild than in Wales, but warmer and bluer, too. There's the food, too. Fresh, seasonal, abundant and cheap. Figs, cherries, peaches, avocados. The food is a luxury in itself. But I'm missing the company of like-minded people and I keep hoping, keep trying, keep reaching out, as much and as often as energy allows.

When I spot a new local Meetup for women entrepreneurs, I go along, fresh from our makeshift bath and with clean-smelling clothes. I feel like a bumpkin coming down off my mountain but it's worth it to find myself in a room full of intelligent, funny women. I still have no idea how I will make a living, or which of my skills will come to be valued in this new place, but in this room, with these women, I can at least start to own my feelings of vulnerability. As we share our stories, a striking sense of solidarity emerges. Few of us feel we belong here. Most of us are in exile from somewhere - burned out from corporate careers or from the sheer effort of living in a world that has too often rejected what we, as women, have to offer. Like me, many have arrived on the tail of their partner's job and have yet to discover their new purpose.
The group grows, nurtured through workshops delivered by members themselves. We explore fresh approaches to business and personal growth. We honour collaboration, mutual support and intuition. This is entirely in keeping with the paradigm of the heroine's journey. Instead of killing the dragons we encounter - either internal or external - whether they show up as inner critics or outward competitors, the feminine way is to befriend, or collaborate. I suppose if women had to rely on the strength

VILLA MIMOSA

required for killing dragons, we would never reach our goals but it is something else, too. Put simply, perhaps the feminine way is more peaceful.

In one workshop, I am asked, "What is it that you really love to do?" It feels like a confession to say that I love to meditate. Why is it so hard to give ourselves permission to do the one thing we love to do? Buoyed by the women's support, I open a Meetup group and on Wednesday mornings, make a spot on the beach to meditate to the sound of lapping waves. I'm still wondering how this little sangha will develop when news of Christopher Titmuss's Agents of Change programme arrives in my inbox and in a moment of rare clarity, I sign up. The course, to be held over four weeks in Germany, is an intriguing mix of social action and meditation. It's just what I need to improve my skills and boost my confidence and I will emerge with a qualification that might be useful if I want to teach mindfulness in schools. Whatever the justification, for once, something in me is yelling an enthusiastic "Yes!"

I'm not yet making a living, but in addition to this small move towards doing what I love and hopefully making a difference in the world, I'm comforted by Su Dennett's words about the household arts. Free from work outside the home, I have time to grow vegetables in our small garden and when I discover and join a community *huerto*, it adds value far beyond what we can grow, bringing me home both to the soil and to the group of people who share that gentle space.

Creating a home economy is about so much more than money. It's about connection, mutual care and reciprocity. I am beginning to create a lifestyle here which feels congruent with my values and principles, closing the gap between my inner and outer worlds. Spending time in nature. Growing food. Being careful with resources. Supporting local enterprise. As well as contributing to my mental and physical well-being, I feel the beginnings of belonging.

Catalunya's long summer days produce many kilos of juicy, ripe tomatoes and more cucumbers and courgettes than we know how to eat. I make sauces and passata, pickles and chutneys. We brew kombucha - the fat, waxy scobies floating in large glass jars of sweetened tea. Hand-inscribed labels declare that our produce is made at 'La Mimosa' and I feel the appreciative gaze of my grandmother upon me.

Slowly but surely, step by step, I am creating what Estés might call a handmade life. It's a life to which my grandmother would have felt akin and I feel the grandmother in me seeking self-expression. Finding my way as a young elder, no longer youthful but not yet with the gravity of old age upon me, I bring what knowledge and wisdom I can. Husband is working hard, spending long hours after work mastering basic plumbing, tiling and carpentry, mostly from YouTube tutorials. He finds a local solar installer to help him fit a few panels. We're not off the grid yet but a few panels give us a bit more resilience. As for me, I do become a little handy with a saw, but am more excited to discover a skill for designing spaces, a boldness with colour and a sense of style of which I was not previously aware. When I signed up for the Agents of Change course, I felt that life immediately took on a new sense of direction. So much so that when the time finally comes to go, I begin to doubt that doing the course is really necessary. The house has hot water and we have found a carpenter who has built us a beautiful, comfortable platform bed and installed a proper kitchen. I have some friends and a growing sense of community. Every day, life feels more cosy and familiar and leaving for Germany, it is like I am leaving a home.

The course is held at a Buddhist retreat centre in the countryside near Düsseldorf, for two weeks in June and two in October. In the months between, a further shift happens in me. Whereas in the beginning I feel shy, unsure and am easily triggered, the second part uncovers a new, quiet confidence. Each morning I wake before dawn to deliver a yoga class, something I haven't done for some time. I am reminded with a flush of joy how teaching brings me delightfully back in contact with the flow of life.

VILLA MIMOSA

Christopher guides the group with a lifetime of skill. He was ordained as a youth, spending ten years as a monk in Thailand and since then, has devoted his life to the twin callings of teaching and social change. In the meditation room and about the retreat centre, he cuts a Leonard Cohen-like figure in smart British-gentleman-style waistcoats teamed with brightly coloured, long Indian shirts. He runs a schedule which is exacting, but which also leaves room for responding to feedback with spontaneity. In the mornings, we dive into the inner world of contemplation and meditation - using additional tools like journalling and writing to help us listen to ourselves. In the afternoon, we engage with the outer world, testing our voices as speakers and facilitators. Learning how to both initiate and navigate difficult conversations, I discover again how listening to others is so vital. As the world around us becomes increasingly fractious, these skills are more and more in demand.

Together, we are academics, artists, writers, teachers and people in business. The youngest is not yet twenty, the eldest over eighty. What we have in common is a commitment to co-creating a more peaceful and sustainable world and the course is designed to help us find our own unique way of doing that. It's challenging, but with each passing day I feel more and more alive. Isn't this what they say to those who are lost? To ask not what the world needs of you, but to ask what makes you come alive and go and do that?

The landscape around the Pauenhof retreat centre is flat, but not featureless. Mornings are misty, hung with dense moisture as night dissolves into day. Afternoon walks take us out amidst agricultural crops. Towering corn, tall broad beans and bright yellow rape. The window of the meditation room looks out onto huge fields of potatoes, so that when my mind seeks distraction, I find myself gazing at industrial-size sprinklers, lumbering determinedly back and forth. Sometimes, a group of us slink off after lunch and go swimming in a nearby lake. Sliding into deep, cold water clears the head and leaves the body refreshed, ready and alert for an evening

125

schedule of dharma talks and inquiry. Water, it's always water for me.

In the evening sessions, Christopher offers inquiry as a kind of performance, in the same way that Carol did on that retreat in Australia. Inviting a questioner to the stage, he holds a space for them to uncover their own answers, offering gentle but firm attention while they plumb the depths of their mind. The weave of dialogue, the perfect balance between concentration and surrender, something magical is happening. What emerges is truth - sometimes difficult and often infused with emotion, but Christopher has a way of always holding it with compassion. Christopher inspires me, but it is the women that teach alongside him that intrigue me most. It is they that offer me a role model, with their gentle humour, grace and ease. They offer a feminine aspect to the practice to which I can aspire. When Shelly Sharon invites an evening meditation in the reclining position, Christopher is concerned that people might fall asleep. "But if they fall asleep", says Shelly, "they must be tired!"

Barefoot in nature, Germany

Chapter 16

What the World Needs Now

"The wisdom is in the group."

Years ago, I made a film for the monks living on Caldey Island in Pembrokeshire. Women are not really allowed into the monastery, but somehow, it was me that ended up recording them as they went about their daily lives, speaking to them about their vocation. I remember Father Daniel telling me how Cistercian monks take a vow of place, promising to remain in the same monastery, with the same Brothers, for the rest of their lives. He called it "putting down roots in order to bear fruit."

In a humble illustration of the frustrations and joys of spiritual practice, Father Daniel shares the irritation he feels when listening to the monk behind him who always sings out of tune, but also how good it feels, at 4am prayer, to offer the elderly Brother beside him a shoulder on which to sleep. In this way, he models effortlessly how to own both our weak points and our strengths. Faced once more with the inner work that needs to be done, I recognise a tendency for me to get stuck in denial.

"You have issues with commitment," says Shelly and immediately, I feel defensive. "Surely not. I've always been somebody who commits to things!"

But of course, she is right. I'm terrified of committing to living in Spain.

HIRAETH

Putting down roots in Catalunya feels like a betrayal of Wales. It feels as though I am abandoning both my land and my son, who wants to have a grandmother around for his children. What's more, it's a betrayal of my own expectation that I will one day re-join my community in Holts Field.

In an exercise designed to address this hesitancy, Shelly asks me to list what is important to me. Then she asks me how I could make time for these things during my week. Putting this schedule into practice will mean more walking, more meditating, more writing, and so in spite of my resistance, I find myself embracing this small discipline. I note that I did not list money as a priority, but that I thrive under the light of validation and I enjoy the feeling of being able to really help someone. To relieve even a tiny bit of suffering. The big picture still feels overwhelming, but the acknowledgement of what is important to me helps me to put one foot in front of the other. What I do not see then is how Shelly is showing me how to practice Rumi's *hundred ways to kneel and kiss the ground*. She is putting the sacred back into my life. She is showing me the Way.

By the time September comes around again, I feel bolder and am able to approach a local school. I'm seeking work, but more than that, I'm seeking connection to my local community. Audrey, the headmistress of The Olive Tree School, is open-minded and in fact, a bit of a radical. She started the school in her own home eleven years ago and was soon forced to find bigger premises. Audrey invites me to begin a Mindfulness Club and we start meeting on Tuesdays after school. We also open a space for staff for a little yoga, massage and inquiry. It's another small step which, like my 'important things' timetable, helps me settle into something of a routine. At some point, it feels right to begin inviting groups to meet at La Mimosa. Up there in the trees, this small, simple, recycled home offers a different perspective on life. The positive responses to our simple lifestyle infuse me with a sense of hope. We created this. It was hard work, but we did it.

When a safe space is held, with clear, loving boundaries, creativity naturally arises. Offered this kind of space, the children in the Mindfulness Club move quickly through boredom towards fresh ideas and activities. They perform plays, write books and invent new games. Adults, too, become playful in this space. Faces relaxing, shoulders dropping, they seem to breathe more freely.

Holding a safe space for adults helps to interrupt the swirl of thoughts. Lucid responses drift up from murky depths and problems, as if from nowhere, discover a solution. Tuning in to the body, to the movement of emotions, to what is important, somehow this opens a door to fresh ways of seeing. Reflections from one individual often chime perfectly with another, weaving us all in an intricate web and demonstrating how, though we appear to be separate, the truth is something else entirely. Time after time, our deep interconnection becomes evident. With our gathering, and in the light of kind attention, moments of profound wisdom arise. Ah-hah moments. Moments of enlightenment.

I like to quote the words of Glen Ochre, co-founder of Commonground intentional community and the Groupwork Institute of Australia. Activist, counsellor, social worker and feminist, facilitation was at the core of Glen's work. When I met her, she had just published her book *Getting our Act Together* and at the same time, had been diagnosed with terminal cancer. I knew her for just over a year and during that time, worked with her family to make a documentary telling her life story. [22] Glen's enthusiasm for facilitation led her to coin a few choice sayings, such as : "The world needs good facilitators" and "First facilitate yourself". But my favourite of Glen's sayings is "The wisdom is in the group."
This last one reminds me that when I am wearing the hat of a facilitator, what I do or say is not the most important thing. What is more important is to get myself out of the way and let wisdom emerge.

It feels very natural when my friend Esther and I begin to hold a women's circle. Esther is a somatic bodyworker and voice coach and she and her partner Marc sing together in a kirtan group. I work with them to make a little film that is as beautiful as their music and in this act of co-creation, a friendship is created too. There's a patch of ground in front of the house that has been holding out for a purpose, which we now make a space for ceremony. Enclosing it for privacy, we hang lanterns and fairy lights, arrange logs around a central fire pit and build an altar from found objects. At the entrance, I place an elder plant, taken as a cutting from Can Masdeu and now standing as a protector of the threshold. Elder is a tree often known in Celtic mythology as a symbol of the cycle of life and death, as it roots and regrows so readily. From flower to fruit to bark and root, elder is a source of powerful medicine. It links me back to my garden in Wales, to my grandmother and to the aunt who passed on my grandmother's recipe. Perhaps, in time, this tree will give us elderflower champagne! In a final flourish, along the threshold step I paint the word *croeso* - the Welsh word for welcome.

On the night of full moon, a circle of women gather to perform a ritual given to me by Ruth, a Canadian woman with native American ancestry. Her people used blue corn as an offering, but I find myself bringing lavender from my garden. When someone asks me the significance, I don't immediately know, but later I understand what lavender means to me. I see how this fragrant, pungent plant also links me back to my ancestry. To my grandmother, who made little perfumed bags to keep moths from our clothes. Lavender is calming and has cleansing properties, so is a symbol of purification. Because it grows freely in the place I now live and because of the link to my personal history, it feels powerful to offer this plant for use in ceremony. Beyond the ordinary realm of existence, ritual and ceremony invite us to take part in the magical web of unseen connections, making it possible to deepen our feeling of belonging. To the land, to each other and even to ourselves.

Slowly but surely, I am finding my place in Spain and the things that are helping me are the very things that helped those communities I visited in Australia. La Mimosa is not part of an intentional community, but we do form a unique settlement of only nine homes, huddled up here on the mountainside. We have meetings to help resolve problems and from time to time, host each other for a party or social event. If one of us is in trouble, we know we will do our best to be there for each other. On a wider level, I have this community of women, with whom I am forming deep alliances. Just as with those Australian communities, these connections develop strength through the power of familiarity and sustained intention.

Filmmaker, writer, yoga instructor, bodyworker, meditation guide. How are these talents best expressed and what kind of life do they ask me to live? Is it possible for me to make a living from these skills? To help me answer this question, I find myself returning to the concept of right livelihood.

The Old English origin of the word livelihood describes it as a 'way of life', from līf 'life' + lād 'course'. Attuning to right livelihood, we are led to address the whole experience of life. What makes it lively? The idea of right livelihood in a western economic context was perhaps first mooted by E.F. Schumacher in the book *Small Is Beautiful*. It was introduced to me in my twenties by my first yoga teacher, Margery. Now ninety years old and recently seen on TV doing the splits and talking about mindfulness, Margery drew on many sources for her classes. With her, we explored right livelihood as a way of making a living based on the principle of *ahimsa*, or non-harm. Right livelihood led me to train as a yoga teacher and strongly influenced my work as a documentary filmmaker. What I'm asking now, twenty years later, is how does right livelihood affect my current decisions? And hey presto, just as has been demonstrated for me so many times before, when the student is ready, the teacher appears.

Jaya Ashmore lives in Catalunya but I first met her on one of her teaching trips to Melbourne. When I left Australia, I was hoping to connect with her but almost as soon as we arrived, life took her off to live in India. In some ways, that all seems irrelevant, as her mentorship programme is being held online. I find myself meeting virtually with people in Israel, the United States and ironically, Australia. Jaya's teachings are free of charge, with an understanding that participants will contribute dana - a expression of appreciation and generosity according to what we can afford. This system of exchange is common in the buddhist traditions, but it is likely that human beings all around the world have always bartered in this way. In Indian cultures, it is often taken to mean charity, but in Jaya's translation, the Sanskrit word *dāna* means 'seed', which helps me see how our gifts support something precious to grow. A system like this goes beyond swift monetary exchange. It requires that we build relationships underpinned by trust and faith.

Jaya has relied on this way of being throughout her adult life. She says that for her, it represents a radical alternative to consumer capitalism, creating connections and community in place of individualism. Modern culture is quick to tell us the benefits of giving, yet slow to recognise the value of receiving. With practice, I start to see how they go hand in open hand.

Experimenting with dana challenges the perception that more is always better. It asks that I slow down, aim not always for quantity, but be more appreciative of quality. It questions the nature of enoughness, and opens an inquiry into the universal laws hidden beneath constraining ideas of scarcity and plenitude. In opening my hand and heart to offer, somehow, receiving is also made possible. By accident or design, this wisdom is missing from Western understanding.

Moving towards this kind of livelihood brings with it a gratitude not only for students and participants but also for all my teachers. For Jaya and Christopher, Shelly, Carol and Jess, for Ruth and for my first yoga teacher, Margery. Sensing the wealth of wisdom and experience behind me, I begin to feel part of a noble lineage.

I've often wondered why I had to wait. Why I had to spend that time wandering in the wilderness. But even a cursory study of the world's

WHAT THE WORLD NEEDS NOW

religions will tell you why a seeker needs to experience the deep unknown. Why the journey calls her to descend.

Arriving in Spain I was left with very few points of reference. My sense of identity fell away and I was tumbled into an emptiness that had me tugging my clothing to see if I still existed. When familiar forms crumble and we are left staring into the void, what is there to catch our thoughts and ideas? Without work, family, friends, community, or a sense of purpose, my mind flailed, grasping at past and future for something on which I could hang my hat. Of course, as the teachings insist, grasping only makes it worse, so, using what tools I had, I practiced opening to the present, with its eternal, uncomfortable unfolding. Home was no longer just in Wales, nor was it in Melbourne. Home was in both these places and now in Catalunya, too. My longing for security was a longing for certainty, but perhaps the only certainty in life is change, and how do we get comfortable with that?

Christopher Titmuss insists that humans have become too attached to the comfortable. Our desire to avoid suffering has been exploited by those who would manipulate that desire for their own ends. In the process we have lost our connection to what is really important. So what IS really important? What does the world need now?

My inquiry partner is a man living in Sydney. From our opposite sides of the world, we have tuned in online for this exploration. We agree, naturally, that what the world needs now is love sweet love, singing a few lines of that famous song and having a chuckle together before settling down to our task. We agree our time frame and our question, and that he will go first.

I pull focus, drawing my mind in from distractions, resting my body back and down, holding still, concentrating on what he is saying, on the way that he is saying it. When seven minutes is up, we swap roles and it is his turn to listen. The air between us goes quiet as we shift our attentions - he towards me and me towards my inner life. A few cars pass on the road below my house and the open door lets in a breeze, ruffling papers on my desk. These noises bring my attention into the room, but I plunge deeper, directing my mind closer to my heart. I am listening for words, images, or simply a sense of knowing.

Moments ago, this man in Australia spoke passionately about the threat of climate change. Australia has suffered severe bush fires again this season and his area just experienced several days over 35 degrees. "And it's almost winter!" he cried. My mind flits back to those oven-baked Melbourne days. Lying listlessly on the sofa, curtains drawn to keep the cool inside. Or else cycling by the river, air so hot and thick it barely registered a breeze on my bare legs.

"We need to address our tendency towards greed and ignorance" he said then and now, a response arises, emerging with a clarity that brings a feeling of confidence.

"Greed appears to me as an attempt to satiate an insatiable hunger" I say, "The hunger gives rise to physical discomfort that we try to dislodge with other comforts. Food, alcohol, sex, work, success, consumption..." The words are a flowing, streaming consciousness. "In an addictive way, we keep reaching for more, even when we understand it will not satisfy our longing and that it serves neither ourselves, nor our relationships, nor the environment upon which we depend. In our haste for pleasure, we too often discard the things of substance - the things that nurture the internal life, that speak to spirit and soul. Soul food."

There is silence while I meet the space. While a breath that seems to have been held for a lifetime releases and my shoulders tingle with relief. I wait for more words to come.

"Instead of more", I wonder out loud, "can we learn to say enough?"

I hear myself say the word and it wants to be said again. I need to not only say it, but to feel it. To know it. For myself, first, but also for those with whom I share this world. Enough. The word circles, lands and stills. This sacred space, held for me by a partner on the opposite side of the planet, has offered up a gift. I sense the back of my body on the chair. Feel my

WHAT THE WORLD NEEDS NOW

feet on the ground. A second, deep sigh escapes my lips. I am back in the centre of Australia, lying on the ground in the middle of the desert, knowing all at once that I am a tiny speck and a precious part of the whole. Enough. I have enough. I am enough. To learn when to say "enough" to oneself is to know when to stop. This feels radical. But also, and equally radical, another expression comes. "Enough is enough." To know when to say this is to know when to say "stop". This enough speaks of self-care but also of boundaries. There is the enough of "yes, this", but also, the enough of "no, not that."

As well as boundaries, 'enough' chimes with the experience of waiting. It speaks of patience, perseverance and acceptance in the face of the unknown. It speaks of practising contentment and making do - ideas that my grandmother would have taken for granted a mere two generations ago.

'Enough' invites me to pause, slow down, to enjoy what I have. In 'enough', there is less striving, less grasping and less comparing. There is a settling back, an allowing, a sense of surrender. There is a coming back to the now, to what is present, to the place I always find myself. This refuge. This resting place. This home inside.

Dharma Yatra, France

Chapter *17*

Walking On

"Being guided from a deeper place."

It is a Wednesday at the end of January when the cat arrives. By strange coincidence, it is exactly five years to the day since we left Wales for Australia. The Welsh weather comes with him and it rains solidly for days, which is unusual in this part of Catalunya. If Shanti the cat were a person, he would have been disappointed. "But I moved to Spain for the sunshine!" he might have said. Instead, he seeks out his 'spot' and stays there, more or less, until the rain stops.

Husband is ill with the 'flu, so he and Shanti lie around, snoozing amicably. Between the weather, the cosy woodburner and the task of caring these two beloveds, I do indeed feel that I have enough. The scene in the house is so familiar, it's as though I have finally managed to re-create the handmade life I left in Wales a full five years ago. It was a life I didn't want to leave and had I known how difficult the journey would be, I might have sent Husband away alone. Yet even as I think this, I can hear the gods and goddesses chuckling.

"It was obvious!" they cry. "How could you not see?" And looking back, I can see. A woman in mid-life, with a grown son and a comfortable life? "She was asking for it" they cackle. But I really wasn't, except that I had

HIRAETH

opted many years before for the red pill, for the road less travelled. I had several times before followed the call of spirit and turned my life upside down, shaken all the pieces out onto the floor, jumbled them around like a scrabble player preparing for the next round and then started again, to see what I could make with my new set of letters. Australia challenged me, but I managed to play a good hand. Then, upon moving to Spain, the letters were once again scattered.

Who am I? Where am I going? These questions can be asked throughout a person's life and each time, a different response emerges. How can we respond in a way that brings freedom? To borrow some words from Jaya, we might answer best when being 'guided from a deeper place.' To follow our intuition involves giving more time and space to the practice of listening to and heeding our inner wisdom. When we open our eyes and ears, we begin to see clearly the way things are and this opens the door to insight. To wisdom.

If there is a golden elixir, I most often find it in the spaces in between. In between words. In between breaths. In between worlds. This is the space where magic happens. From this space, creativity arises. This is the space between action and reaction, between contact and response. It is also the space between not knowing and knowing. Between uncertain and certain. Between unseen and seen. This is the space we can find so difficult to navigate, because it seems at first as though either nothing, or everything, is happening. If nothing is happening, we become bored, apathetic or insecure, whereas too much happening leads us into anxiety and overwhelm. With calm curiosity, we can witness all these experiences, taking action to make change where change is possible. Enjoying ease when ease arises. Knowing what truly makes us happy and knowing, too, that what brings discomfort will point us faithfully towards our wounds. Wounds which, in turn, offer an entry point to freedom.

As human beings living in such uncertain times, perhaps drawing close and being curious is exactly what is needed. Just as by tuning in to our own pain, we stand at a doorway to personal truth and freedom, so listening to the pain of another enables us to support them more effectively. Could listening to the planet lead us to hear the earth's own truth?

In the modern world, it's easy to see how disconnection happens, but that word *hiraeth*, embedded in the ancient language of Welsh, suggests that humans were susceptible to this long before industry, technology, politics and circumstance caused separation. Finding our way back to a state of connectivity - or even more, to a state of communion - is a practice, a way of being in the world. With each breath, we take in the possibility for life. Releasing the breath, we can accept the inevitability of death. In the space between, we can connect.

***

It is the time of ripening. During the day, thoughts keep time with the rhythm of one hundred pairs of feet tramping upon hot, dry ground. Prickly husks of nuts, the swish of red-brown leaf litter, the airborne scent of freshly-harvested lavender and the determined breathing of one hundred walkers keeps me company as landscape shifts between vast mountain reaches, shady forest groves and open stony hillsides. The temperature gauge hovers near thirty-four degrees - hot for this part of southern France, even in late July. Behind my small moonstruck tent, pears drop to the ground with gentle thuds, reminding me that at home in Spain, tomatoes will be piling up in the kitchen and Husband will have his work cut out to keep up with them. How is the cat coping with this heat? I can't help but worry. He's a Welsh boy, but even in Wales the summer has been unusually warm. Hovering alongside insects in humid air you can hear the confused whisper of *climate change*.

This yatra is in its eighteenth year, though I first heard of it only a

HIRAETH

few years ago, when Jess came from Australia as one of the teachers. I promised myself that once back in Europe, I would come and here I am, accompanied by Linda, a new friend and neighbour. Christopher is teaching and it is good to hear him again and to see Joe and Robert, some colleagues from the Agents of Change course. It's a surprise when I also see Mirabai, sister of Mitra, my neighbour at the Cairo flats in Melbourne. Mirabai is a filmmaker too, so aside from the family connection, we have lots in common. As well as these familar folk, there are a hundred and twenty other adults and twenty-two children moving around the French countryside in an ingeniously-organised fashion. We hike from early morning to late afternoon in our long, silent, snaking row and in the evening, we meditate and listen to dharma talks from Christopher and other presiding teachers. We're a group of travelling pilgrims. A mobile sangha.

It was this way in the time of the Buddha, when he taught outside in the groves of India, nature providing both container and support. We live a similarly simple life, catering only for basic needs. There is a sheltered kitchen where a dedicated team prepares healthy food from local ingredients, a tented dharma hall offering shelter from hot sun and passing rains, and pit toilets dug by generous members of the site crew. As with most retreats in the Insight tradition, we all pitch in with tasks. It keeps the costs down and helps create community, equality and appreciation. Every few days, the whole camp infrastructure moves, to provide variety in the hiking tracks but also with the idea of limiting our attachments. Moving home like this is not easy for me and with each fresh campsite, I find myself disoriented. How I love to have a home! Is this not the lesson, though? To be nimble in the face of change? To move with the flow of life? It is not for nothing that pilgrims wander.

Resting on a grassy patch, I take up a meditation position, allowing my back to soften and letting go of the feeling that I am still wearing my backpack. Shoulders drop a little. Jaw slackens. Eye-senses turn inward.

WALKING ON

This combination of physical exercise, nature and contemplation quietens my mind and I drop quickly into wide-open awareness. Though I can't help but notice a twinge or two in my aching back, I feel peaceful and content.

What the yatra demonstrates is how community can come together quickly. Through common purpose and values, shared activity and interdependence, we rely on each other to get through each day. When one person is unable to contribute, as happens when my back finally gives in and I am forced to take a day of rest, there is enough goodwill for someone to step in and complete my tasks, and enough love left over to offer me some much needed healing.

Lying prone, receiving the kind attention of my companions, I am forced to surrender not only to the hand that life has dealt me but also to the gifts that are offered. In this context, it is not so difficult. I can see the input I make to help this camp happen and have myself offered something to people who are suffering. Here, it is simple to see the ebb and flow of karma To see the give and take of the big picture. It's easy to receive when I have only recently freely given. How do I maintain this vision of completeness in the outside world? There, it is harder to see the connection between one thing and another. Giving and receiving are most often separated by time and space. How, there, can I maintain this faith?

The yatra operates solely on dana, relying on contributions from participants. There is no charge aside from a basic registration fee and it would be possible for me to accept all of this bounty and walk away. Every year, despite insecurity and anxiety, the organisers trust that expenses will be covered. Each year, their faith is vindicated and the yatra continues to thrive.

What do I take away from this, apart from a sore back and worn-out sandals? I take a sense of belonging. I take a full heart, a vibrant soul and inspiration to help me take the next steps in my life. If it is possible to create this ambitious pilgrimage each year in the French countryside solely on goodwill, love and commitment, then what other miracles might be possible?

***

The Heroine's Journey

Afterword

Asked whether this is a self-help book, my considered answer is both yes and no. While I feel human beings have done quite enough helping ourselves, mostly at the cost of other species and the Earth as a whole, it's true that we do need support. Yet I can't envision a way of helping ourselves that does not also include helping each other or helping our environment, because are we not inter-connected? Any self-help programme of activity will quickly reveal the impact of our actions on others and on the world around us, so maybe it doesn't matter where we begin our healing journey. There are doors and windows everywhere, if only we can learn to see.

At the heart of this journey is listening. Deep, embodied listening. Listening to ourselves - via meditation, inquiry, awareness and creative practices. Listening to each other, through dialogue, group and shared community. Listening to the land, through our ability to make ourselves quiet and be touched by nature's cycles of pure being. We have a lot to learn, but fortunately we are also surrounded - everywhere and on all levels of being, by teachers.

With this last point in mind, I give thanks to all my teachers, who show up in all their forms, wherever I go. May I have the humility to recognise you, the wisdom to hear you and the courage to follow your guidance.

HIRAETH

It is dark when I hear the Call.
Moon, who stalked my sleep with suggestion
bids me rise, and so I do,
with reluctant feet and cautious heart,
trusting that the Way will be revealed.
Step by steady step, an ascent.
Until, with apparent ease,
mountain gives birth to the generous sun!
Does it end there? Not at all.
Cold hard stone illuminates with honeyed grace.
Cool and shady, hot and sharp.
Sometimes I lose my footing.
But following the prints of those before,
with those behind to watch my step, I arrive.
Back at the place from where I first set out.
Awake.

Notes and Resources

1. *The Bell Jar (1963) by Sylvia Plath* was one of the first fictional representations of the personal effects of depression to be published, but it had a hard time seeing the light of day because of the stigma of association. It was dismissed by its first potential publishers as "disappointing, juvenile and overwrought", but subsequently has become lauded for its moving account and is often studied in classrooms.

2. Statistics suggesting that mental ill-health is a growing global phenomenon are not hard to find. One useful resource is :
https://ourworldindata.org/mental-health.
This graph, for instance, shows how anxiety-related disorders have risen since 1990 :
https://ourworldindata.org/mental-health#depression

3. Heather Jo Flores is a feminist writer and permaculture teacher, best known for her book *Food Not Lawns : How to Turn Your Yard Into a Garden and Your Neighbourhood Into a Community* (currently awaiting reprint). In her MFA thesis, Heather explored the phenomenon of the Heroine's Journey and teaches a short course online for those who would like to know more.
https://www.heatherjoflores.com/

4. The One Planet Development planning guidance began as Policy 52, under which the Lammas ecovillage was created. You can find the One Planet guidance on the Lammas website:
http://lammas.org.uk/wp-content/uploads/2013/03/one-planet-development-guidance.pdf
Further extensive detail and discussion of this policy going forward is offered by the One Planet Council:
http://www.oneplanetcouncil.org.uk/

5. The Centre for Alternative Technology is at the forefront of eco-building techniques, not only in the UK, but worldwide. Whether a fun day out, an exciting group visit, an eco-hideaway, a short course or fully-validated MSc study programme, CAT is a reliable combination of lived experience and up-to-date information, delivered in an accessible way.
https://www.cat.org.uk/about-us/

6. I lived in Cairo flats between 2012-2015 and for an inner city development, it had a surprising sense of community. This was greatly supported by the design itself and showed how important it is that human connection is considered when imagining how people will live in a place.
http://architectuul.com/architecture/cairo-flats

7. At the time of writing, we are experiencing the highest-ever number of air travel journeys per day. Sites such as https://www.flightradar24.com/ will show you every plane in the air at any given time. Aeroplane fuel is tax-free, making it hard for other, less carbon-hungry forms of transport to compete, but as evidence and urgency grows, so does pressure to change our habits.
https://www.wanderlust.co.uk/content/to-fly-or-not-to-fly/

8. The land of Australia has been inhabited by Aboriginal people for between 50-70,000 years. There are over 250 language groups, though

NOTES AND RESOURCES

modern settlement has disrupted much of their useage. The Boonwurrung clan lived on the land now known as Melbourne and Port Philip Bay.
"The Boonwurrung people continue their tradition as the proud custodians and protectors of these lands from the Werribee River to Port Phillip Bay to Westernport Bay to Phillip Island and all the way to Wilsons Promontory."
http://www.boonwurrung.org/

9. The Urban Coup are a group of Melbourne-based people with a vision for creating a city-based community founded on co-housing principles. In 2018, they submitted planning permission to build "29 apartments over 6 storeys including a mix of 1-bed, 2-bed and 3-bed apartments. The development will include common spaces, both indoor and outdoor where residents can meet, socialise and share meals and other activities and events. Common spaces include a kitchen and meals area, common laundry, and multi-purpose spaces for music, workshops, art and crafts and for guests."
A second Urban Coup development, further out in the suburbs, is still seeking suitable land.
http://www.urbancoup.org/

10. After beginning life as a small community co-op and resource centre, Commonground is meeting the requirements of its second generation of leaders by embracing a model which opens the doors to a wider circle of stake-holders. In addition to a residential aspect, Commonground emphasises its role as space-holder for courses, land-based learning and generator for group development for a just and sustainable world.
http://www.common-ground.org.au/community

11. Moora Moora is home to around 50 adults and 20 children. Built on ecological principles, the community features several different modes of eco-construction, including rammed earth, cob and straw bale buildings. They have regular open days and host workshops, conferences and other community-supporting events.

http://mooramoora.org.au/

12. Murundaka have pioneered an all-rental co-housing model, based on a principle of affordability and long term home security. There are 20 households organised around a central communal space, with shared facilities. It is home to 30-40 people between birth and 60 years old. Co-founder of Murundaka Co-Housing and Earth Co-op, Iain Walker, died in October 2019. His vision and contribution to this movement improved the lives of many people and he will be greatly missed.
https://www.murundakacohousing.org.au/

13. Earth Co-Op is the holding agency for Murundaka Co-Housing, but before that, existed as a co-operative providing secure housing for eleven households.
https://www.murundakacohousing.org.au/earth-coop

14. https://aiatsis.gov.au/publications/products/case-summary-mabo-v-queensland

15. Robin Clayfield is a pioneer in the field of social permaculture and has run her group programmes since the late 1980's.
https://dynamicgroups.com.au/

16. David Holmgren, along with Bill Mollison, is one the founding fathers of the permaculture design system. He lives with his partner Su Dennet in a beautiful demonstration property north of Melbourne.
https://holmgren.com.au/money-vs-fossil-energy/

17. NAIDOC originally stood for National Aborigines and Islanders Day Observance Committee. The term is now representative of a movement for First Nations recognition across Australia and in particular, a week-long celebration of cultural events during the month of July.
https://www.naidoc.org.au/

NOTES AND RESOURCES

18. The world needs architects who embrace the need for ecologically-friendly, healthy building techniques. Architecture Architecture are involved in the design of co-housing developments across Melbourne, demonstrating an understanding of both people and place. http://architecturearchitecture.com.au/

19. The Enclosure Acts permitted the removal of land in Britain from common use and the displacement of the people who lived and farmed on it. The Acts were part of a far-reaching land grab designed to move property into the hands of the wealthy and leave the poor with no option for survival but the work for the land owners in fields and factories. https://www.fff.org/explore-freedom/article/enclosure-acts-industrial-revolution/

20. *Deep Listening* is a 60-minute documentary exploring some long-term ecologically-based intentional communities in Australia and in particular, the ways in which they handle conflict. The film also visits an Aboriginal community to further explore the ideology known as *dadirri*, or deep listening, as practiced with land and people alike. http://livinginthefuture.org/deep-listening.php

21. Karinna Nielsen gives an interpretation of Innanna's descent in *"Inanna Passes through the Gates"*: https://www.karinnanielsen.com/lemurian-goddess-wisdom/46-inanna-and-her-journey-into-the-underworld

22. Glen Ochre was co-founder, with Ed McKinley, of the Groupwork Institute of Australia. You can buy her book *Getting Our Act Together* and *Child of the Earth*, the documentary I made about her life, from their website : https://groupwork.com.au/

***